TAROT FOR BEGINNERS

A PRACTICAL AND STRAIGHTFORWARD GUIDE TO READING TAROT CARDS

DAVID HOFFMAN

© Copyright 2019 by David Hoffman

All rights reserved.

This document is geared towards providing exact and reliable information with regards to the topic and issue covered. The publication is sold with the idea that the publisher is not required to render accounting, officially permitted, or otherwise, qualified services. If advice is necessary, legal or professional, a practiced individual in the profession should be ordered.

- From a Declaration of Principles which was accepted and approved equally by a Committee of the American Bar Association and a Committee of Publishers and Associations.

In no way is it legal to reproduce, duplicate, or transmit any part of this document in either electronic means or in printed format. Recording of this publication is strictly prohibited and any storage of this document is not allowed unless with written permission from the publisher. All rights reserved.

The information provided herein is stated to be truthful and consistent, in that any liability, in terms of inattention or otherwise, by any usage or abuse of any policies, processes, or directions contained within is the solitary and utter responsibility of the recipient reader. Under no circumstances will any legal responsibility or blame be held against the publisher for any reparation, damages, or monetary loss due to the information herein, either directly or indirectly.

Respective authors own all copyrights not held by the publisher.

The information herein is offered for informational purposes solely, and is universal as so. The presentation of the information is without contract or any type of guarantee assurance.

The trademarks that are used are without any consent, and the publication of the trademark is without permission or backing by the trademark owner. All trademarks and brands within this book are for clarifying purposes only and are the owned by the owners themselves, not affiliated with this document

.CONTENTS

INTRODUCTION 1
HISTORY OF TAROT READING 4
STARTING OUT YOUR JOURNEY TO TAROT READING 8
ASSOCIATED TAROT RITUALS 12
ASKING A QUESTION 15
THE TYPICAL TAROT DECK 17
KEEPING A TAROT JOURNAL 20
THE MEANINGS OF TAROT CARDS: THE MAJOR ARCANA 23
    0 – THE FOOL 24
    I – THE MAGICIAN 26
    II – THE HIGH PRIESTESS 29
    III – THE EMPRESS 31
    IV – THE EMPEROR 33
    V – THE HIEROPHANT 35
    VI – THE LOVERS 37
    VII – THE CHARIOT 40
    VIII – STRENGTH 42
    IX – THE HERMIT 44
    X – THE WHEEL OF FORTUNE 47
    XI – JUSTICE 50
    XII – THE HANGED MAN 53
    XIII – DEATH 55
    XIV: TEMPERANCE 57
    XV – THE DEVIL 59
    XVI – THE TOWER 61

XVII – THE STAR 63

XVIII – THE MOON 65

XIX – THE SUN.. 68

XX – JUDGEMENT 70

XXI – THE WORLD 72

THE MINOR ARCANA 74

ACE OF WANDS.. 75

TWO OF WANDS.. 77

THREE OF WANDS 80

FOUR OF WANDS... 82

FIVE OF WANDS... 84

SIX OF WANDS 86

SEVEN OF WANDS 88

EIGHT OF WANDS 90

NINE OF WANDS.. 92

TEN OF WANDS 94

ACE OF CUPS.. 96

TWO OF CUPS.. 98

THREE OF CUPS.. 100

FOUR OF CUPS... 102

FIVE OF CUPS 104

SIX OF CUPS 106

SEVEN OF CUPS 108

EIGHT OF CUPS 110

NINE OF CUPS.. 112

TEN OF CUPS.. 114

- ACE OF SWORDS ... 116
- TWO OF SWORDS ... 118
- THREE OF SWORDS ... 120
- FOUR OF SWORDS ... 122
- FIVE OF SWORDS ... 124
- SIX OF SWORDS ... 126
- SEVEN OF SWORDS ... 128
- EIGHT OF SWORDS ... 130
- NINE OF SWORDS ... 132
- TEN OF SWORDS ... 134
- ACE OF PENTACLES ... 136
- TWO OF PENTACLES ... 138
- THREE OF PENTACLES ... 139
- FOUR OF PENTACLES ... 141
- FIVE OF PENTACLES ... 143
- SIX OF PENTACLES ... 145
- SEVEN OF PENTACLES ... 146
- EIGHT OF PENTACLES ... 148
- NINE OF PENTACLES ... 150
- TEN OF PENTACLES ... 152

COURT CARDS ... 154
- THE PAGE OF WANDS ... 157
- THE PAGE OF CUPS ... 158
- THE PAGE OF SWORDS ... 159
- THE PAGE OF PENTACLES ... 160
- KNIGHT OF WANDS ... 162

KNIGHT OF CUPS 163
KNIGHT OF SWORDS... 164
KNIGHT OF PENTACLES... 165
QUEEN OF WANDS 167
QUEEN OF CUPS 168
QUEEN OF SWORDS 170
THE QUEEN OF PENTACLES 171
KING OF WANDS.. 173
KING OF CUPS.. 174
KING OF SWORDS 175
KING OF PENTACLES 176
FINAL NOTES.. 177

INTRODUCTION

When a lot of people hear the word 'tarot,' the first thing that comes to their mind is usually along the lines of 'black magic' or 'fetish' or 'charms.' Even though the concept of fortune-telling and divination has been a big part of Tarot for centuries, tarot is still a lot more than that. Tarot is essentially a way of life on its own; a form of culture, a historically-rich practice that has helped to create incomparable bonds, forge paths, and completely change lives.

Tarot reading is a special type of practice in which an individual, known as a reader, directed by intuition and skill, interprets cards drawn from a deck of specialized cards known as tarot cards. They use the knowledge derived to answer a specific question, usually about his own future, or the future of someone else who asked them a question.

However, tarot cards are not only meant to be read. Since the early 18th century, records of a specific card game known as 'tarrochi' have been noted. This game is a typical card game like modern day bridge, except that tarot cards are used in playing it.

Tarot reading is a practice with a history that dates as far back as the 15th century. Even though records show that tarot reading and even the tarot deck first appeared in Europe, a lot of myths and narrations suggest that tarot originated from Egypt. According to Antoine Court de Gebelin, a 16th century French clergyman, the Tarot deck and the practice of Tarot reading are actually related to the Egyptian book of Thots, one of the scriptures that form the bedrock of Egyptian Theology. Gebelin suggested that four of the major Tarot cards actually represented four of the core principles of Christianity – Temperance, Justice, Strength and Prudence.

Whether you believe that tarot can help you add meaning to your life and aid you in making key life decisions or not, tarot is actually immense fun on its own, even without reading the cards for any clandestine meanings. Playing tarot with friends and family can help strengthen existing bonds and create new ones.

Tarot can also be incredibly relaxing, and it forces you to think deep; to relate specific images and core meanings of cards to particular real-life situations, and draw connections that may help you gain insights that you didn't have before. Believe it or not, for centuries, experts have actually appraised the amazing soothing and calming powers of tarot that make it the perfect process to help you keep your head clear so you can view situations from perspectives you previously didn't even know existed.

By sharpening your mind to help you ponder extensively, tarot not only improves your critical thinking skills, it also guides you on your path to self-discovery and heightened spiritual awareness. By helping you to make more use of your intuition than your analytical mind, tarot helps you to discover a part of you that the modern world forces you to repress; the spiritual part of you. With both the analytical and intuitive segments of your mind fully developed and honed with the aid of tarot, you are not only able to see everyday issues from diverse perspectives, you actually get to become a more well-rounded individual.

If you, as an individual, are more adventurous than the average mind (and since you are reading this book, I assume you are), then you are definitely curious about how a deck of cards with images and core meanings can help to foretell a person's future or help a person to make decisions. As a matter of fact, whether tarot is going to work for you as a guide to making important personal decisions actually depends on you. You, as the person asking the question are the most important factor in the tarot equation.

For a tarot divination to work, whether you are doing a personal reading, or you are having someone do the reading on your behalf, you have to be absolutely open-minded for a tarot reading to work for you. The difference being receptive to a wide range of possibilities and being open-minded makes, is it actually allows you to reach down into the deep recesses of your mind to ask important questions, and frame them in a way that should be done. When a card is drawn, or a spread is created, your open-mindedness is going to aid you in relating the message delivered by the cards to your personal life, and help you make any related important decisions you need to make.

When you are not open-minded, however, you are not likely to be willing to even deeply ponder on the message related by the cards. You'd be more concerned about proving the cards or the reader wrong than finding a way to connect the reading to your personal life. In the ancient practice of using tarot cards for divination, there were varying theories about how the supernatural forces that guided the positioning and the picking of the cards actually worked.

Some schools of thought believed that the cards served as repositories of spiritual power that simply got arranged in a specific fashion based on the specific problem the querent was trying to solve. Another school of thought believed the tarot readers were the ones who held the supernatural powers that enabled them to draw the right cards from the deck or position the appropriate ecards into appropriate arrangements to allow for an accurate reading. The common factor between both theories, however, was there was a supernatural force in play, and the picking of the cards was never random.

Learning to read tarot cards is a gradual process; a process that cannot be rushed under any circumstance. Learning to read tarot cards can be likened to building a house. First of all, you need to learn how to make your bricks, and then you need to assemble those bricks to form basic structures. Then you need to learn how to incorporate appropriate additions, and from there you can be on your way to erecting your own unique superstructure; a creation with your own unique, individual imprint.

However, to learn the basics, you need a guide, and the purpose of this book to guide you through your early stages of learning to read Tarot cards. As you progress in tarot, your interest is likely to get even more rekindled, and then you can seek out more advanced material on the use of tarot cards for personal divination. There is a lot to be learnt about tarot reading as a science and as an art, and it promises to be an exciting, mind-blowing experience. Welcome aboard!

HISTORY OF TAROT READING

As a beginner in the art of tarot reading, for you to fully appreciate the beauty of Tarot, and for you to properly understand its global cultural significance, it is quite essential for you to be at least slightly familiar with its history.

The origin of the tarot deck and the art of tarot reading is actually shrouded in mystery and not fully understood. Since tarot reading is such an old art which has been in existence for at least half a millennium, it's easy to see why there would be different accounts about its actual place of birth, and its original inventor.

While the fact that a unanimous agreement on the origin of tarot may never be reached may be a tad frustrating for some tarot enthusiasts, the fact that its origin is actually mysterious, to say the least adds to the intrigue of the art, making it even more breathtaking and scintillating to learn. So, as you go through the pages of these book and learn about the ancient art of Tarot reading, have it at the back of your mind that you are undergoing a process millions of people have been undergoing for over 500 years. Now, how is that for being a part of history?

According to records from European museums, tarot decks have actually been in existence since the 15th century, as evidenced in the tarot decks available in the museums' collections. These decks are nothing like modern tarot cards; they are sophisticated and highly elaborate – they are simply miniature works of art dripping with gold, probably made for the pleasure of royalties at the time.

According to some accounts from Egyptian mythology, tarot cards were actually created by the Egyptian god, Thoth. Thoft was said to have gifted the art of tarot reading to man from the great Egyptian pyramids to serve as a source of guidance and light for his subjects, and to enable them to find direction when they felt lost. It is speculated that somehow, the culture of reading Tarot cards may have died down among the Egyptian population, only for it to surface in Europe in the 18th century, courtesy of the Gypsies in their fancy caravans who were an exotic sight to behold in ancient Europe.

When the Gypsies came to Europe with their simple yet fancy cultural inclinations, they quickly infiltrated the very fabric of the European society. Soon they were soon found in a lot of major European cities, especially in France. These Gypsies did Tarot readings for people in a similar fashion to the astrologers who read people's palms at carnivals and quaint little roadside shops today. In return for their services, the Gypsies collected silver pieces they used for day-to-day living, The Gypsies were extremely simple, yet incredibly profound people who discovered the secret to happiness was not accumulating wealth and rooting yourself to a point, it was in putting smiles on people's faces, while moving from city to city to find more faces to put smiles on. They didn't have a lot, but they had enough to leave an indelible imprint in the books of history.

Since Tarot reading encompassed the use of cards in divination and fortune-telling, several religious factions soon came out to condemn the practice of Tarot reading among the Gypsies, calling the Tarot cards 'the Devil's picture book.' This notion is one that has been effectively passed down through several generations over the centuries, and one still held by some religious groups to date.

While everyone has the absolute prerogative to determine their own religious beliefs, it still feels pretty absurd that an art that has helped to define the way of life of a people (the Gypsies), and has helped to bring so many smiles to so many faces, create so many bonds, and even helped, in its own little way to shape history as we know it is seen to be something evil.

If there is anything evil about Tarot, it would be its dangerous power to addict; once you start, there's no going back. You'll keep hankering to know more, and the more you unleash your intuition, the more capable you will be of understanding the intricacies of life from different profound perspectives.

In all, it is important to note the aim of Tarot is not to corrupt your religious beliefs or make you practice voodoo. Not at all. Tarot aims to help you find inner peace as you progress on your journey of life. Tarot aims to help you find a channel through which you can unleash your powerful intuition that the modern world has effectively helped you cage through the instilment of rigid rules and regulations right from your childhood. Tarot enlightens you and helps you to think outside the box. Tarot is all about harmony and flowing in sync with the universe – it's basic principles are freedom and imagination.

The most reliable account of Tarot's history is it made its first appearance in Europe in the 15th century where the Tarot cards were used in a game called Tarrochi, an ancient form of the card game of bridge. This account is actually believable because the images used in the cards that made up the decks found in 15th century Europe are actually similar to the images etched onto the stained glass windows of European cathedrals and public buildings built around that period.

Even though Tarot cards were only played for fun at first, the possibility to use them in conjunction with a sharp intuition, an open mind, and perhaps some supernatural powers in fortunetelling soon led people to start using Tarot cards for divination purposes. Antione Court de Gebelin was one of the first public critics of Tarot reading – calling it an occultist practice only fit for heathens, despite the fact he also believed that some of the cards portrayed principles that formed the core of Christianity.

The first Tarot deck made specifically for the purpose of divination was first made by a Parisian seed salesman known as Jean-Baptiste Alliete, who wrote under the pen name, Eteilla, which is simply his last name spelt backwards.

The beginning of the 20th century was a remarkable period in Tarot history. In 1909, Arthur E. Waite, a member of the Golden Dawn, a secret English magical society, published the first standardized deck of Tarot cards, and called it the R.W.S (Rider-Waite-Smith) Tarot deck. The paintings on the cards were made by Pamela Colman Smith, and that Tarot deck is the most widely accepted and soled Tarot deck in the world till date.

Over the years, slight modifications have been made to improve user experiences, but the original Rider-Waite-Smith deck remains the foundation upon which all these developments have been made. In 1943, Aleister Crowley collaborated with the talented artist Frieda Harris to create the Thoth Tarot deck, the second most popular Tarot deck model in the world.

In the earlier parts of the 20th century, fortune-telling Gypsies still used Tarot cards for divination, and even though the Gypsies have faded away with time, the practice of reading Tarot cards still remains highly appreciated and widely practiced.

In the 1960s, important books that helped the average man with no previous contact with Tarot to have comprehensive knowledge about the art were published, further exposing Tarot to different parts of the world. Eden Gray published 'The Tarot Revealed' and 'Mastering the Tarot', both in the 60s. Gray's teachings of tarot reading encompassed the interpretations used by fortune tellers to read the cards, and the practices of secret societies in ancient Europe in using the cards for divination. Other important Tarot books that helped to lay the foundation for Tarot literature were '78 Degrees of Wisdom' by Rachel Pollock and 'Tarot for Yourself' by Mary. K. Greer.

Over the years, since its introduction, the basis upon which Tarot reading is built has shifted gradually from fortunetelling to psychology. In the first centuries of Tarot reading up till the beginning of the 20th century, the principle of Tarot reading existed on the basis of people's general belief in fortunetelling. Back in those days, people were actually open to idea of a supernatural force helping to reveal hidden information through the card readings. However, with the passage of time, has come the evolution of the society, and people no longer hold the kinds of beliefs in the supernatural that they used to. Therefore, for Tarot reading to survive as an art, its foundation; its basis had to undergo a paradigm shift from fortunetelling to psychology.

Currently, the principle of Tarot reading is based on a delicate psychological understanding by card readers and querents alike. People in the modern day understand that they have their freewill, no matter what the card readings are, but they still believe that considering the results of a card reading with an open, intuitive mind would allow them to be able to find solutions to their problems from perspectives that could not be reached by mere analytical thinking. That notion is the current bedrock of Tarot reading among most modern adherents.

However, for any entity to truly thrive and survive through the ages, it must continue to evolve. The truth, however, is people have come to accept psychology FULLY as the basis for the existence of Tarot reading in the modern dispensation, thereby effectively blocking all routes through which tarot reading could further evolve in the future. The basis of tarot reading has evolved from being a type of fortunetelling to being a function of psychological beliefs – it has to keep evolving to keep growing.

Therefore, instead of just accepting psychology as the supreme basis for the functioning of Tarot reading, it would make a lot more sense instead, if we were more open-minded as adherents of this ancient art, to allow different thought patterns to run. People should be allowed to believe whatever they want, so that when the society evolves, tarot reading can evolve along with it.

STARTING OUT YOUR JOURNEY TO TAROT READING

We all start our journey to tarot in different ways; different circumstances lead different people to tarot reading. Inevitably, people are going to view the very practice of tarot reading from different individual perspectives. The most difficult fact to accept about tarot reading, however, is the fact there is no absolute right or wrong way to carry out specific actions, or to make certain deductions from tarot cards.

Unlike other more accurate scientific fields, tarot reading is an art that has thrived over the ages on generating controversies in interpretations; bringing people together using differences in their reasoning. So, the way you are going to understand how the reading of a particular card or spread appears to your own peculiar situation might differ slightly from how even your reader would see it.

They key to being a great tarot reader in the long run, therefore, is for you to first look deep in the recesses of your own mind, find yourself, and come to terms with who you are. You need to realize exactly who you are, underneath the cloak of educational backgrounds, social class and all those cloaks we use to mask our real selves in the modern society. You are not your occupation or job description, you are not your position in your family, you are not the role that the society has foisted on you.

You must go back to the very basics of your consciousness and discover who you really are and the ideals you hold dear. Discovering yourself will help you to have an independent voice and a self-reliant thought pattern that will be able to help your intuition bloom. Once you as a person are in perfect harmony with your intuition, then reading the cards and relating them to your personal life becomes easier.

Discovering yourself will also let you find out you are intrinsically different from everybody else. Who you are fundamentally as a person differs from what people think you are, and it sure differs from who other people are. Therefore, since we all different on a very primal, basal level, it is not expected for our intuitions to work the same way. What your intuition regards the interpretation of a card to mean in your personal situation is likely to be slightly different from what someone else would think if they got that particular reading in your same exact situation. So, self-discovery will let you understand who you are, and will let you come to terms with the differences that exist between yourself and others.

Now that you have understood that the basic requirement is knowing who you are to enable your intuition to bloom unrestricted, the next step is for you to learn the basics of Tarot. For a tarot reading to be carried out, five basic pre-requisites must be in place. First and most importantly. There should be a reader. If there is no reader, then exactly how is the interpretation of the card going to be determined? So, a reader has to be in place to examine the cards drawn and the spread created, and to guide the person who asks the question on the core meaning of the reading produced. This leads to our second most important factor, the querent. In Tarot literature, a querent is simply the person who asks the question (or who makes the query). In circumstances of personal divination therefore, the reader and the querent are going to be the same person. So, the querent is the one who is seeking an answer to a burning problem.

The third pre-requisite is the question itself. This is the most important thing the querent has to possess for a tarot reading to be successful – a concise, clear-cut question that has been decided on in advance or on the spot. For a querent to be able to relate a tarot reading to his own personal circumstances, the question asked has to be as concise and unambiguous as possible.

The next most important pre-requisite is the deck of cards. There are different types of tarot cards in existence currently, but the most common and most widely accepted tarot deck is the Rider-Waite-Smith tarot deck. The original version of this deck was first created in 1909, and its simplicity and conciseness has endeared it to the hearts of many tarot readers over the years. This has made it the deck of choice for both avid tarot enthusiasts and beginners who are just starting out in the game of tarot reading.

The average tarot deck consists of 78 cards, the structure of which will be extensively discussed in another section before the meaning of each of the 78 cards is examined in detail. The whole tarot deck can be divided into two major sections, the major arcana, or the major mysteries, and the minor arcana, or the minor mysteries. The cards in both sections of the deck will be explained in detail as we move on.

Finally, a spread is the last important pre-requisite for a reading to be completed. A spread may be an arrangement of cards picked out in a particular fashion based on the direction of the reader's or querent's intuition. In other types of readings, the spread may be a single card pulled randomly from a deck or from a random pile of cards. Whatever form it takes, the most important thing to note is that the spread is the card, or sequence of cards that is interpreted to give an answer to the question asked by the querent.

Even though a lot of tarot readers practice personal divination in the modern dispensation, back in ancient Europe, there were huge concerns about the ability of readers to be objective when seeking answers to their own questions from the cards. So, when carrying out a personal divination through a tarot reading, as both the reader and the querent, you need to strive consciously during the course of the tarot reading to remain as objective as possible when carrying out the reading.

Of course, as stated earlier, there is no specific way to interpret a spread. People examine core meanings, and then relate them to their own specific situations based on their individual convictions. So, whether you like it or not, your personal convictions about that question you asked will come into play as you seek answers from the cards. It is now up to you as a reader to look deeply at the core meanings of the cards in your spread, and make an objective deduction based on your intuition, and not a deduction that aligns with your wishes.

Since the heyday of Tarot reading, the practice has never been seen as a form of inquiry from an absolute supernatural source. Tarot reading have always been regarded as a way of providing a mirror for us to gaze back unto ourselves, our unique predicaments, circumstances and situations and reflect deeply to come up with intuitive deductions and solutions. The aim of tarot is to help you reach into the deepest recesses of your mind, and relate the tarot reading you have done by yourself, or the one an expert reader has just done for you to your unique circumstances.

It's actually that simple. Having to distill the path to the solution of your problems to just one image or a few sequential images allows you to think deeply from a unique perspective. See how the core meanings of the card relate to you, and begin to work out a simple, basic solution to your problems. Tarot helps to eliminate complexities by forcing you to come down to a basal level when attempting to solve a problem. Instead of engaging your analytical mind and trying to find various complex solutions to mostly simple problems, tarot brings your intuitive mind into the picture and allows you build your solutions from the simple to the complex phases, which is the most efficient mechanism of problem solving.

Contrary to popular opinion, you don't need to have studied the entire tarot deck to be able to perform a simple reading. As has been reiterated severally in this book already, the key to a successful tarot reading is your intuition; the limitless power of your mind. So, as a total novice with no prior knowledge of tarot, you can still carry out an effective tarot reading using the power of your intuition. All you have to do is get your deck of cards (you can do that right now if you have your deck with you), think of a particular question, pull out a single card (we don't want any complications yet), and then think of how the image on the card relates to the question you asked.

You can just write down the first couple of things that comes to your mind. It might take a while for you to be able to effectively establish a connection between the question you asked and the image on the card you pulled. That's where the power of your intuitive mind comes in. The more you ponder intuitively on the image, the clearer the path between your tarot reading and the question you asked becomes to you. It's so simple, yet so unbelievably powerful.

Finally, to conclude this section, we'll be looking at how to appropriately read a spread. The spread, as has been discussed earlier is the layout of the cards that allows the reader to provide an answer to the querent's question using his interpretation of the core meanings of the cards and the sequence in which the cards appear. Sometimes, the sequence of the cards may not be put into consideration, it all eventually boils down to your intuition.

Most tarot readers like to use a three-card spread. The first card represents the events of the past, the second represents the events of the present, while the third represents how the past and present will lead to a particular future occurrence. For some readings, only once card is used, and in some readings, more than three cards are used. No hard and fast rules apply.

ASSOCIATED TAROT RITUALS

First of all, relax. The rituals here are not the types you see in movies where you have to draw mysterious signs on the ground, wear a hooded robe, place candles at specific spots and then begin to recite incantations while waiting for a huge, scary gust of wind to blow. As fascinating (or downright petrifying) as that would have been, tarot reading does not involve fetish ritual proceedings in any from. 'Ritual' in this context is a set of actions that you carry out before a tarot reading to help calm your mind and 'activate' your intuitive capabilities.

As mentioned earlier, we live in a world where everything is all about analytics, data and structured information. To cope in the real world, your analytical mind needs to constantly be at work; you need to analyze how much you have spent on gas, how many more years you have left to pay off the mortgage, how many calories you have consumed in a day…the list is endless. But for an effective tarot reading, you will need more than just your analytical mind, you'll need your intuitive mind on board. So the rituals are just a process of helping you clear your mind, and usher in your intuition to lead you through the reading.

It is essential to note that carrying out a ritual is not a compulsory prerequisite for an effective tarot reading session. If you feel you can utilize your intuition efficiently without needing to prepare your mind in advance first, then by all means, fire down. But over the centuries, most people have found it extremely helpful to have a specific routine that helps them get prepared to engage their intuitive capabilities before carrying out a tarot reading.

Your ritual should preferably be a consistent practice. It can be as simple as taking a few deep breaths and closing your eyes to enable you to calm your mind, to using velvet, silk, crystals, candles and incense to create a specific type of atmosphere you feel helps you get in touch with the deepest recesses of your mind. When it comes to tarot rituals there are no specific standard procedures. It's all about figuring out what works for you and harnessing it to the fullest to enable the delicate balance between your analytical mind and your intuition to be established. Once you feel you have reached that state of delicate balance, then you may proceed with your tarot reading session.

It is very important that your ritual procedure be a series of steps you are completely comfortable with; both mentally and physically. If you are allergic to something, it doesn't make sense to use it because you think it would let you be at peace. If something scares you, then it doesn't make sense to include it in your ritual routine either. You'd want to be clear-headed, not apprehensive while carrying out your tarot reading.

However, as long as you are comfortable with a particular series of steps, then by all means, carry on. Even if it is carving out specific signs on sand and lighting candles and saying whatever incantations come to your mind, as long as the ritual process makes you feel at peace and unlocks your intuitive capabilities, by all means, fire on.

A great part of most people's tarot rituals is saying prayers. If you believe in God, or the existence of a supreme supernatural entity, then you can ask Him for guidance and direction as you prepare to proceed to seek answers to your burning questions. Communicating with an invisible divine entity not only helps to calm you down and improve your intuition, it also allows you to be collected enough to frame your question properly. When you are praying, you are likely to say your question out loud; to ask God for help. Therefore, praying helps you to frame your question right without any ambiguities.

Another key part of most rituals is deciding exactly how many times you would shuffle the tarot deck before carrying out your reading. The amount of times you shuffle the deck will eventually have a direct impact on what your final reading is going to be, so it is extremely important for you to be clear-minded as you decide exactly how many times you want the cards to be shuffled.

During the process of preparing your mind to carry out the reading, it is also important for you to decide whether you as the reader will be the one to shuffle the tarot cards, or if you will be doing it with the querent, or if only the querent will be responsible for the shuffling. As stated earlier, there is no absolute right or wrong way to do these things; it all comes down to personal traditions, and of course, intuition. So, while carrying out your ritual, it makes sense to visualize the tarot reading in your mind in advance, and decide exactly who would be doing the shuffling of the cards.

It is believed by a lot of tarot experts that a unique, temporary and mysterious bond actually exists between the deck of cards, the reader and the querent during the process of the reading. The open-minded atmosphere helps to connect them, and as the reader and querent open up their minds to the possibilities of the reading's results they find themselves working together on a subconscious level to find a solution to the querent's problems.

ASKING A QUESTION

The question is the most fundamental part of the tarot reading process. The question asked by the querent gives direction to the reading, and allows the reader to attach a meaning to the cards he is trying to read. There is a wide misconception that the question has to be verbally asked. This is not so. If the question is about an extremely sensitive matter the querent is not open to discussing with the reader, then the querent simply has to ask the question in his mind, and tell the reader that the question has been asked.

The tarot reading then proceeds, the cards are drawn and read, and the core meanings of the cards drawn are communicated to the querent. From the meanings of the cards, he can deduce the answer to his questions. If the question is not communicated expressly to the reader, it might make things a little complicated, but it doesn't make the process of tarot reading impossible. It only means the reader has to explain the various dimensions the reading may take to the querent.

Apart from serving as the focus of a tarot reading, a question, especially an expressly asked one, gives the reader an insight into the mindset of the querent. The form the question takes would allow the reader to understand if the querent is the type of person who is more inclined to believe in the power of destiny or the influence of freewill. The querent's belief system is going to have a lot to do with how the cards are going to be read.

If a person asks, "Will I get a great job after college?" for instance, that question automatically portrays that person as someone who believes more in the power of destiny; a person whose mindset is fixated more on how the flow of the universe affects his life rather than how his own efforts dictate his future. Of course, this is not to say the person who believes in destiny would not understand that freewill and actions will have huge effects on his future. He just prioritizes destiny over freewill. Recognizing this fact will enable the reader to prove an answer that correlates to the querent's mindset.

On the other hand, if another querent asks a question like "What do I have to do to get a high-paying job after college?" then it is obvious that this querent believes more in the influence of freewill in dictating the future than destiny. This individual is all about taking his fate in his hands rather than letting the universe's flow decide it for him. Recognizing this fact also helps the reader to read the cards in such a way to provide the perfect answer to the querent's question.

Therefore, the art of tarot reading does not involve reading the cards only, it involves reading the querent too, whether we, as readers are carrying out personal divinations, or if we are doing readings for others. It is important to understand the querent's mindset and use that as a catalyst to providing an answer the querent can work with in the long run.

After the rituals and asking the question, then the cards have to be cut. The process of cutting the cards involves the querent or reader (depending on the decision reached during the ritual) dividing the deck of cards into piles, usually three piles. The piles may then be picked one after the other and restacked severally until the shuffler is satisfied. When the shuffler's intuition tells him it is time to move on, then the cards are dealt.

Once again, there are no hard and fast rules about dealing the cards. Most people prefer to just pick the cards on top of each pile, arrange the top cards in order, and carry out the reading straightaway. Some people prefer to pick the cards and turn them upside down before finally revealing each card and carrying out the reading. Other people do not even pick the top cards at all, some pick cards from the middle of the deck; it all depends on the reader's discretion.

If the cards are dealt facing upwards, it allows the reader's subconscious to start analyzing the reading early, even before the complete spread is fully dealt. However, some readers favor the 'face-down' approach to ensure that their minds are clear as they deal with the cards without having to think about the cards that have already been dealt. Once again, it's a game of personal choices.

In some readings, cards are not actually even cut into piles. What is done is the cards are spread randomly all over a table or platform, and the reader simply picks specific cards out of the mass of cards to carry out the reading. This method, is however criticized since the reader may actually choose cards that convey a positive message instead of the whole process being as random as possible.

In all, the most important factor in choosing cards to be read during a reading is spiritual guidance. Be in touch with the deepest recesses of your being, let your intuition roam free. You'll feel a lot more enlightened and in touch with your clairvoyant side if you have done your rituals right, and you can be sure you actually feel a comforting internal force guiding you as you pick your cards.

THE TYPICAL TAROT DECK

As mentioned earlier, tarot cards are divided into two major sections, the Major Arcana which reveals major mysteries, and the Minor Arcana which functions in the revelation of minor mysteries. There are seventy-eight cards in all. 22 cards make up the Major Arcana, and they are numbered from 0 to XXI. Each of the cards of the Major Arcana has a specific name, unlike the cards of the minor Arcana which are usually described by their position in the suit and the suit they are found in. The first card of the Major Arcana is the Fool, numbered 0, and the final card numbered XXI is named 'World.' All the cards of the Major Arcana suit are trump cards in the game of 'Tarrochi,' except the Fool card.

When we say that the cards of the Major Arcana help in the revelation of major mysteries, it means reading the cards of the Major Arcana helps to indicate a major life change is going to occur, or a major life decision is going to have to be made soon. The difference between the cards of the Major and Minor Arcana is the Major Arcana helps to reveal the coming of hugely significant life-changing events, while the cards of the Minor Arcana simply help to reveal minor mysteries like everyday occurrences.

More often than not, the cards of the Major Arcana reveal mysteries beyond our control; events that are likely to serve as important milestones in our journey through the Earth. Hence, Major Arcana cards may not be drawn so often, but when they are drawn, it means something big is coming. So, if a divination is made, and a Major Arcana card shows up, it is unlikely your actions are going to lessen the possibility of that event happening. However, knowing about the possibility of that event occurring in a particular sphere of your life (depending on the question you asked) will put you in a position to be able to handle the coming events with adequate preparedness.

The remaining 56 cards of the typical Tarot deck constitute the Minor Arcana. The Minor Arcana consists of four major suits numbered from Ace to Ten, and four additional court cards per suit, bringing the number of cards in each suit of the Minor Arcana to fourteen. The four suits of the Minor Arcana are named according to the intrinsic meanings of the cards they contain. Each if the suits of the Minor Arcana are named according to each of the four elements that were believed to constitute the universe in ancient times – fire, water, air and earth.

The suit representing the element fire is known as Wands, the one representing water is known as Cups, the one representing Air is known as Swords, and the one representing Earth is known as Pentacles. Depending on the tarot deck being used, alternative names may be used in the nomenclature of the suits of the Minor Arcana. The Wands suit may be known alternatively as Rods, the Cups suit as Chalices, the Swords suit as Spears and the Pentacles suit as coins. It is not he name that a particular suit is called in a deck that matters, what matters is what element of the universe the suit represents.

In addition to the ten fundamental cards (ace to ten) of each suit in the Minor Arcana, there are four additional court cars. Where the fundamental cards help to reveal minor, everyday mysteries, the court cards actually represent people in our lives. This actually makes court cards quite difficult to read. Depending on the circumstances surrounding the question, it might be tough to identify the particular person in your life that a court card refers to. Each of the four court cards in a suit are named in order of significance, the king, the queen, the knight, and the page. Alternatively, the court cards may also be referred to as the Father, Mother, Son and Daughter cards in some particular tarot card decks.

So, while the court cards may be a bit hard to read if the direct meanings of the cards are being used to try to identify a particular person in a querent's life, it gets easier when the court cards are used to interpret the roles that specific individuals play in the querent's life, under the circumstances that led to the asking of the question.

Therefore, when a king card comes up, instead of looking for someone gigantic or who has a particular eye color, the person who fits a particular king-like role in the circumstance that prompted the question is interpreted as the person that court card is referring to. Simply put, instead of tracing court cards to physical characteristics, court cards are used to fish out people who are likely to pay particular roles in a particular circumstance instead.

So what exactly do the suits of the Minor Arcana generally mean? The Wands suit, that represents the element fire, stands for passion, intensity, energy, fiery determination, drive, and even in some cases, anger and vengeance. Fire is basically interpreted as something intense, something unstoppable. When a question is asked and a card from the Wands suit is picked, it usually has an implication that refers to a person's aspirations, career, projects, or serious undertakings.

The Cups suit represents the element water. This suit is usually interpreted in the context of emotions and usually holds information regarding relationships, dreams, intuitiveness, love, and even friendships. The Cups suit can help a querent to answer burning questions about his relationships and his emotional life in general.

The Swords suit represents the element air, the most evasive element of all. Air usually represents things that are delicate and hard to keep stable. The swords suit usually gives insights as to information regarding logic, thinking, communication and even problem-solving. These are aspects of a person's life that might be quite fleeting and tough to deal with – just like Air.

Finally, the last suit in the deck is the Pentacles suit representing Earth. The earth is solid, grounded and stable. Cards of the earth suit usually enlighten a querent about issues grounded in reality such as his finances, resources and his health. These prospects are not fleeting or evasive, they are non-abstract. They are facts and figures that can be examined, reviewed and worked on. The Pentacles suit helps to provide information on subjects that are a real part of human lives.

KEEPING A TAROT JOURNAL

When learning anything, it is important to keep a record. Right from our days as kindergarten pupils, we've been trained to always keep records of what we learn. That's because when you learn something, and you do not have the means to revisit that imbibed knowledge, it simply fades away from your memory over time. However, when you keep going back to what you have noted, that knowledge tends to become ingrained in your long-term memory over time, eventually becoming a part of who you are.

How you choose to keep a record of your tarot knowledge is going to depend on your own personal preferences. Factors such as long-term availability of your records, ease of accessing your records, and transferability of your records may be important factor to consider before choosing a journaling method.

A lot of people, even in the modern era, tend to favor the traditional notebook as a means of maintaining a journal. This method is convenient and efficient, notebooks are affordable and readily available, and you can easily refer to your records on the go. Notebooks are small and therefore, mobile, so while you are on the bus, the train or in a taxi, you can easily whip out your tarot reading notebook and go over what you have learnt. It is also pretty convenient to input information conveniently into a notebook. Including images in the notebook is also fairly efficient, except there are no blank pages dedicated for drawings.

Another journaling technique very similar to the traditional notebook is a three-ring binder. I have always preferred three-ring binders personally because you can easily attach more pages of information to particular spots within the book without having to create the mess of stapling or gluing pages together. The three-ring binder also usually has blank pages, making it easy to create any drawings you might desire.

Perhaps the most efficient method of journaling in the modern dispensation is through a personal computer. Inputting information is relatively easy if you are familiar with the computer system, although the average computer system is considerably more expensive than any traditional notebook or three-ring binder. If you are out of power also, you might not be able to get access to your files. If you choose to use a laptop computer instead, you might even have to shell out more money. However, the laptop provides the convenience of mobility and a battery that can help store power.

Whether you choose to input your information into a Laptop of Desktop computer, there are various Cloud storage platforms available in today's rapidly developing technology industry, making it possible for you to store important files on online storage platforms. The advantage of these Cloud storage systems is you can access your information even if your personal computer gets damaged or misplaced. Another advantage of using the Cloud storage systems is you can easily access your tarot notes and drawings on your mobile device or any other computer if you do not have immediate access to your own personal computer.

A mobile phone or tablet is also a convenient means of storing your tarot notes, though it may be quite challenging to input images into your mobile phone, except you choose to download those images online. Even at that, coupling those images to your notes on your mobile phone might still be quite daunting. Mobile phones also usually have limited battery capacities and storage capabilities, making it quite unreliable in extreme circumstances and environment. However, mobile phones can be used to connect to Cloud storage systems to save and retrieve files, and that makes them quite handy.

Storing your files on a blog is an efficient way of sharing your knowledge and development with a group of like-minded individuals who like you, are also passionate about Tarot. While the costs of maintaining a blog and cybersecurity issues might be significant challenges militating against this form of journaling, it is a highly laudable method to enables you to not only learn from your own research, but from the research of other passionate tarot readers as well. Some individuals may not like blogging about tarot because they might want to keep their questions and tarot readings private.

However, journaling about tarot is not just about writing down notes and making drawings. It's also about utilizing your records as efficiently as possible to make you a true master of the art. It is important for you to review your notes from time to time, and if you believe in divination, keeping records may be a good way to keep track of events that you are expecting to happen. Reviewing your notes from time to time will make you gradually develop until you can recollect core meanings of cards once drawn off-hand without consulting any written literature.

To ensure you keep your journal constantly updated and get as much tarot practice as possible, it is necessary for you to do tarot readings regularly. If you can't do readings every day, then endeavor to create a schedule that allows you to do tarot readings at least three times a week. That way, you can keep learning new things about the interpretations of cards, you can hone your intuition, and you can boost your open-mindedness.

An efficient method that can encourage regular practice is just asking a question in your mind, and pulling a card out of your deck at random. Take a few minutes to consider how the card you pulled relates to the question you asked, and write down what your deductions are. If you have the time, you can include an image of the card you pulled and include its core meaning as part of the caption. This way, you keep learning and your journal remains constantly updated. If you just choose to write down the card you pulled, the question you asked, and your deductions, then within five to ten minutes, you are done with tarot reading practice and you can move on with other endeavors.

Another effective method of journaling is freewriting. Freewriting simply refers to the practice of picking a random card that inspires you, and writing about what that card signifies to you. If you feel the card you pulled is symbolic to an occurrence or circumstance in your life at the moment, you may also write about it. The aim of freewriting is to help open up your mind, encourage your creative juices to flow, and of course to help you when you eventually decide to do an actual tarot reading.

You can record your freewriting records in your journal, and if you have a blog, your personal opinions about a particular card and what it represents may be commented upon by visitors to your blog who may gave assenting or dissenting opinions, or who may have something additional to chip into the points you made. Any way you look at it, freewriting is a fast and effective way to help you progress in your studies of tarot.

When doing freewriting and the card you pull is a court card, things can get even more interesting. You are just not thinking of situations in your life the random card has helped you to recollect and put in focus, you can also remember people, perhaps long-lost acquaintances or friends that the image on the card has helped you remember. This may even encourage you to rekindle those old flames and reconnect with long-lost loved ones.

THE MEANINGS OF TAROT CARDS: THE MAJOR ARCANA

You have done an extremely great job following this book so far, and now that all the preliminaries have been covered, you are fully ready to delve into the art of reading tarot cards. In this section, we will be reviewing the meanings of the cards of the Major Arcana, or the Major mysteries. The cards of the Major Arcana are pretty easy to interpret, as they contain images that are extremely relatable. The cards of the Major Arcana usually contain images that depict specific archetypes or mythological roles that are widespread and known to all – for instance the sun, the moon, the fool and the devil.

Archetypes are a grander from of stereotypes; with the aid of the image, you can deduce the role the represented figure plays in the order of events in the universe, and from there, a core meaning of the card is derived. As mentioned earlier, the sighting of a card of the Major Arcana is quite a big deal if you believe in the divination process, and it is sign that something big whether negative or positive is about to go down. Whatever card of the Major Arcana is pulled or drawn; one thing is sure; the coming event is going to change the direction of the querent's life for good.

So, in this section the 22 cards of the Major Arcana will be reviewed. Illustrations of the cards being described will be included to help you as the reader to examine the cards themselves and the meanings we have assigned to them in this book. You can then relate the images on the cards to the assigned meanings, and make your own additional deductions of you have any. You can also begin your tarot reading process from this book. As you read, imagine you have asked a specific question about a major aspect of your life, and that card was pulled. What would your next move be? You can record your thoughts and observations in your tarot journal. Now, let's get cracking.

0 – THE FOOL

This card represents new beginnings, just as it is the first card of the Major Arcana. However, this card just doesn't represent the start of a new phase of life, it represents a tendency to make spontaneous irrational decisions based only on flimsy signs, and without any logical basis. The fool is a person who always has his head in the clouds, and never has his feet planted firmly in reality. The fool's card predicts that the querent is on the way to making a major life-changing decision that has the ability to usher him into an all-new phase of his life, a phase that might have been expected or unexpected.

Either way, the fool's card serves as a caution for the querent not to be foolish as he makes major life decisions. The fool' cards serves to remind the querent to rely on solid facts and figures rather than sentiments and mere hopes. The fool is only motivated by blind faith and spontaneity, the fool lives for the pleasure of the moment and rarely ever stops to consider the long-term effects or consequences of his actions. The first card of the Major Arcana when drawn serves to remind a querent to remain rooted in reality.

While it may be important to take leaps of faiths in our lives at times, this card reminds us not to be like the fool who simply throws caution to the wind and moves aimlessly without any definite direction or destination in mind. It is important to be bold, audacious, ambitious and determined to achieve your goals, but it is also incomparably essential to consider your pros and cons very carefully before making any major, life-changing decisions.

As depicted in the image of the fool above, the fool stands under the sun. This represents optimism, positivity, brightness, and hope. The fool is also looking up towards the sky, meaning the fool is following his dreams and visions, even if he doesn't have a definite plan in mind. He does not mind that he doesn't have a definite roadmap to help him reach his goals, he just wants those goals accomplished at all costs.

Also, in the image, it is obvious that the fool is standing near a cliff. This represents the absence of caution. The fool doesn't realize how close he is to peril, still he leans dangerously close to a devastating fall while basking in the beams of hope and dreams. The overall message communicated by the card is that the fool is an individual who follows his visions – probably visions of immense riches, power or influence without an actionable plan. Due to the absence of a path to this dreams, the fool is always dangerously close to falling off the edge, and whether the fool will realize his goals or not is entirely uncertain.

INTRINISIC MEANING OF THE CARD: The Fool's card simply represents the period before a big decision or life change is made. It reminds the querent to always look before his leaps to avoid falling off the cliff.

I – THE MAGICIAN

The magician represents the creation if change by utilizing a connection with the divine or the supernatural. The magician's card reflects the higher plane of existence is inevitably connected to the lower plane, as is portrayed by the magician holding up one hand, and pointing the other downwards. The magician reminds us that with a connection to the supernatural and a determination to actually create change, nothing is impossible.

The magician's card is therefore a message to the querent that if they want to change the world, then they need to keep the principles of hard work, dedication of resources and sheer will in balance with a relationship with the supernatural, as the happenings in the lower plane (on Earth) are inevitably influenced by decisions made in the higher plane. The magician's card also shows knowledge of the laws by which the universe operates is extremely essential to success.

As can be seen in the image of the magician's card depicted above, there is actually a magician who has one hand pointed upwards, and the other down, showing the connection between the supernatural higher plane of existence and the natural lower plane. This depiction reminds us to always keep the higher plane and the entity who rule sit in focus while pursuing our dreams.

The magician is seen to be holding a wand, a symbol that has been used over the ages to symbolize the power of sheer will. The magician's card therefore serves to remind us that for anything to be achieved, in conjunction with the assent of higher powers, sheer will play a very central role. You must be willing to fight for what you want. You must have a driving force pushing you to achieve your goals; a reason that keeps you going even when the going gets tough. The magician's wand symbolizes the importance of will and determination in the achievement of goals and the leading of a desirable life.

On the other hand, energy is channeled from above to the lower plane. This signifies we are but conduits in this world, despite the fact we have free will and are responsible for our actions, we can also put ourselves in positions to be used as conduits for transmitting the power of the divine onto our own plane of existence. The channeled energy passing through us from the diving can then be used to actually influence the change we desire to see in the world.

Just below the hand stretching downwards, white lilies can be seen on the ground. These white lilies represent the purity of the results of a relationship with the divine. Keeping the higher plane in focus not only helps you to achieve your dreams with help from above, it actually helps you to keep your hands clean without engaging in any misdemeanors while at it. In the end your results and accomplishments are clean and untainted, just like the white lilies that have sprouted from a combination of sheer will and divine powers.

The red roses in the image have been unanimously agreed upon as representations of passion. Apart from divine help and sheer will, passion plays a central role in the success or failure of a person in a particular role, and in life. It's generally easier to muster the will needed to achieve complicated tasks when an individual is actually passionate about a cause, but when the passion is absent, then the will isn't usually natural, it's only forced. And forced will never really endures in the long run.

The red flowers signifying passion there remind us that whatever we do in life to create a change in the world, we should make sure a natural passion is present right from the onset to fuel us through the journey. When the passion is absent from the onset, fake passion will only last so long. And when the fake passion and enthusiasm eventually burns out, then the only thing that follows is despair, and eventually failure.

The double-rounded lemniscate is common in the scientific community as a symbol of infinity. That lemniscate shows that when divine help, sheer will and passion come together, then a person becomes capable of infinite possibilities. It doesn't matter what endeavor you have decided to embark upon, as long as you have those three factors in place, then you will find always find a way to keep pulling through. The good times will help you recharge your faith in the divine, your will, and rekindle your passion, and in the tough times, those three factors will help you to remain standing when others fall.

Finally, a chalice, sword, and a pentacle are also present in the picture. These symbols have been generally accepted to mean resources, and they indicate the important of resources – financial, human and other resources in the actualization of desired change. While divine help, sheer will and passion will set you rolling, eventually, you will need resources to achieve your dreams, because without money for instance, no reasonable change can be created, and without working together with other humans, not much impact can be created either.

INTRINSIC MEANING OF THE CARD: The Magician's card is an indicator of the possibility of a great change that will only happen when divine help, will, passion and resources come together to form an unstoppable alliance.

II – THE HIGH PRIESTESS

The most noticeable thing about the High Priestess card is the fact she is sitting in front of an entrance that represents the threshold to another dimension. Tarot experts have deduced she represents a guard who must let an individual through onto the next level beyond that threshold. However, the ultimate requirement that the high priestess requires is direct experience. In life, we have always heard it from several sources that experience is the best teacher. Therefore, knowledge, insight and wisdom gained from experience tend to be remain ingrained within a person's psyche for far longer than knowledge simply learned from an outsider. The High Priestess demands experience and nothing less, because she understands the critical importance of direct experiences to the human process of learning. When people never get to actually experience things like loss, pain, excitement or danger, they never really get knowledge or information ingrained into the core of their being, and as such they are not permitted by the high priestess to proceed to the next level.

The fact there is a veil drawn across the threshold shows the details about the next level that the querent would be able to access when the necessary experience is gained are hidden. Explicit details would only be available when the querent actually amasses the experience necessary for him to access the next level. So, the basic message is that a next level of achievement is actually possible for the querent, if and only if he is ready to make the necessary sacrifices needed to amass the experience needed to unlock that next level.

The High Priestess is connected with water, and water is associated with constant change. Water flows and this symbolizes that the future is an ever-changing entity. The future is going to eventually be what we make it by the sacrifices we choose to make today. Therefore, the message the presence of the water is trying to pass is that the future is a fluid prospect. If the necessary experiences are gotten in the present, then the future would be bright and stunning. If the necessary sacrifices are not made in the present however, then the future is likely to be compromised.

Several tarot experts have also postulated that the High Priestess card may signify an impending acceptance of the querent into a clandestine or classified society – not necessarily a dark or negative association, but at least a gathering that is not accessible to just anyone. While the association or society may be positive or negative, the point is that before the querent gets admitted, he must pay the necessary price first. The high priestess guards the gate to the threshold, and she will not let anybody through unless they fulfill all the necessary conditions.

The veil in the card is seen to be decorated with pomegranates. This symbolizes the journey of the Greek goddess Persephone, into the underworld. What this symbolizes literally is death. Death is a threshold on its own, and after death, a person gains entrance into a whole new dimension – the afterlife. Now, the kind of afterlife a person gets is going to be determined by the experiences he has amassed during his stay on earth. If he managed to stay on the straight and narrow path, choosing good over evil, then his experiences on Earth would make him eligible to an afterlife of bliss and happiness. If he, however, has lived a life filled with hate, recklessness and debauchery, then he is assured of an eternal vacation in the blazingly hot afterlife that would make the heat of the New York summer look like the Antarctic by comparison.

The Water and the Moon in the image have been postulated to represent a change is definite or unknown. This supports the notions expressed earlier that for an individual to gain entrance through the threshold that the High Priestess guards, then a particular price must be paid. Once that price is paid, then the derails of the dimension beyond the threshold become revealed. The moon and water state that change is imminent. The moon itself is a constantly changing entity that sometimes reveals just as much as it hides, and it is a perfect symbol to signify definite change whose details are not fully explicit.

The fluid nature of water symbolizes that the future is fluid and changeable, and if the necessary experiences are gathered, then a person becomes capable of actually stepping up beyond a threshold to hit the next level. However, if the individual refuses to commit himself to the process of self-development, then the future remains automatically bleak.

INTRINSIC CARD MEANING: The High Priestess card symbolizes a mysterious change whose details are not revealed, that can only be made possible if specific requirements are met by an individual first.

III – THE EMPRESS

The Empress card of the Major Arcana has been reported over the centuries to translate to the beauty of life, nature and growth. The card has also been said to symbolize birth, ripening, and the beginning and peaks of specific life cycles. Basically, the empress card serves to remind us that life is all about the laws of nature, and the querent is assured of bliss and growth when the natural time for it comes. The card also represents abundance and beauty – characteristics of nature that are seasonal. Once again, the querent is being reminded that life is all about changing seasons, and when patience is exercised, the time of drought will pass, and the time of plenty and abundance will come.

While the empress card does not expressly specify that the querent will have to pay a specific price for success, it does signify the coming of a bountiful harvest for a person who has actually sowed good seeds. But now, a person who has planted wheat in the soil does not get to reap barley, does he? So even though the empress card is a symbol of impending abundance and bloom, if the querent has not done anything to deserve the coming goodness and richness, then it is highly unlikely he will be reaping anything worthwhile, or anything at all. That's where the laws of nature come in.

In the image on the card, the empress is depicted sitting on a throne, looking calm, collected and in control. The empress in this situation represents the rules of nature in our journey through life. The rules of nature reign supreme, they are the ultimate laws of the world. And a key rule of nature is that a time will come to sow, and after a while, the time to reap follows. So, if a person has made the right efforts in the past, the card signifies the time is coming for the person to reap the rewards of his past efforts.

In the picture, the empress is also surrounded by pillows and blankets. These items represent opulence and luxury, and show that the coming times will herald peace of mind and bountiful treasures. The querent is going to be happy and satisfied and fulfilled, and the coming period of his life is going to be characterized by the actualization of his dreams. The pomegranates and wheat in the picture signify the coming of harvest – the individual has invested the seeds of time, energy and effort into ensuring that when the time for harvest comes, his rewards would be abundant.

In the image, stars are also present, showing the importance of the passage of time in the affairs of man. There is time to sow, a time to be patient, and a time to reap. Time is central to the achievement of all goals; hence it is highly critical for individuals to pay attention to the timing of their efforts, and to endeavor to remain patient as they hope for the realization of their goals.

INTRINSIC CARD MEANING: The Empress card signifies the coming of abundance and wealth if the querent has actually put in the necessary efforts for him to deserve the riches he seeks.

IV – THE EMPEROR

The Emperor card stands for the entity of a creator and manager of affairs. The emperor represents order, efficiency, prosperity and stability. Unlike the empress that symbolizes the coming of abundance and plenty, the emperor signifies long-term stability and efficiency in the management of an individual's affairs. The emperor represents an epitome of grounded authority, an experienced and seasoned ruler who does not make pronouncements out of prejudice or emotion. The emperor is highly controlled, practical, and organized as an individual. He oversees the affairs of his empire without being too harsh or too meek. He is a representation of balance and firmness.

The influence of a figure like the emperor is necessary for the long-term sustainability of any organization, association or undertaking. While it may be okay to splurge sometimes, and take a break and have fun, the emperor reminds us we must always keep the long-term survival of ourselves and our organization into consideration. The emperor reminds a querent to think beyond the present and focus more on delayed than instant gratification.

The emperor also represents the principle of discipline. Without discipline, an individual is likely to be act in an uncontrolled manner, and that is where failure starts from. The emperor serves to remind us as individuals to be conscious of our responsibilities to ourselves and to those around us to ensure our own long-term happiness and survival, as well as theirs.

In the image on the card, the emperor is shown to be sitting on a regal yet relatively simplistic throne, and the backgrounds reminds an insightful viewer of a desert. Inevitably, the emperor symbolizes the efficient management of scarce or limited resources to ensure fairness and survival.

If your resources are limited and you still choose to squander them instead of looking for a way to manage them judiciously and probably multiply them, then you are going against everything the emperor stands for.

The sun in the background represents logic and rationality leading to long-term progress. The emperor deals in logic, not emotions. He is grounded in reality. He realizes the true situation of things, and he is willing to manage resources, not just for his own benefit, but for the benefit of all parties concerned.

The throne, apart from being simplistic, looks stable, cube-like and sturdy. This represents the stability that the emperor's efficiency and frugality affords him and his subjects. Because he consciously manages his resources and chooses long-term development over short-term benefits, the emperor remains standing even when the shallow thinkers crash.

In all, the emperor card reminds a querent to be responsible and to maintain order and frugality in their lives to ensure long-term prosperity and development. A true empire only endures and grows under an emperor who saves up for a rainy day and manages scarce resources judiciously.

INTRINSIC MEANING OF THE CARD: The querent is being advised to create order and stability in his life to ensure the reaping of long-term rewards.

V – THE HIEROPHANT

When you look closely at the image on the Hierophant on this Tarot card of the Major Arcana, the pope comes to mind. The Hierophant is basically a teacher who lives his life to serve as an example to others. The hierophant represents sanctity and sacredness; truth and light. The Hierophant not only serves to teach people how to walk in the light, the Hierophant actually ensures that every action he carries out and every word he speaks actually conforms to the beliefs that he preaches.

The Hierophant card is therefore about teaching and instruction. However, the style of the Hierophant's teaching is slightly different from the conventional teaching and learning paradigm the world is used to. The Hierophant teaches people to walk in the faith, and he teaches them to do so by using every aspect of his life as a sterling example of exactly how people are expected to behave.

In our lives, especially in the modern society, it is extremely very easy to get carried away by various distractions and sway from our ideals. The Hierophant serves to remind us we should endeavor to live our life to actually serve a higher purpose rather than just to fulfill our own wishes.

In the image portrayed on the Hierophant card, the figure and the setting can be seen to be formal and fairly ritualistic. This points to the fact that for success to be achieved by us as individuals in life, we need a reliable pattern to follow; an everyday routine that helps us to achieve our set goals. The formal setting is also interpreted to mean training, discipline and accountability, all of which are factors essential for success in all fields of human endeavor.

The role of the hierophant is not just to manage and direct like the emperor, but to show the way to true happiness and realization of dreams by his own personal lifestyle, The Hierophant is not much an authority as he is an example. Without training and discipline as individuals, we cannot establish and stick to daily pattern that would ensure success. Instead we would just go along with our whims and desires, and eventually end up disappointed.

The Hierophant's raised hands show 2 fingers pointed up, and two pointed down. Much like the representation of her magician, this symbolizes how importantly sticking to the laws of the divine can help us to live fulfilled lives here on earth. The fingers pointing upwards and downwards symbolize the connection that exists between the higher and the lower planes of existence, and how true success and peace of mind cannot be truly achieved unless an individual maintains a solid connection with the divine, or the higher plane of existence.

The wand in the image on the Rider-Waite-Smith Hierophant card of the Major Arcana depicts the Hierophant holding a wand that's topped with crosses. This serves to represent the relationship between the spiritual and physical realms of life. A lot of people in the modern world tend more towards practicality and rationality and neglect the existence of the spiritual aspects of the universe.

The Hierophant therefore serves to remind the querent to maintain a balance between his spiritual and physical life. While he strives to achieve his worldly goals in his career, relationships and family, it is also extremely important for the querent to remember to maintain his relationship with the divine to keep him pure and truly balanced.

INTRINSIC CARD MEANING: As you go through life, remember to live everyday single day practicing your faith, and as much as possible, let your life a model for others to be able to follow.

VI – THE LOVERS

This particular card represents the complex union of opposites, and how two seemingly different components of life can come to together to produce extremely powerful effects. The overall synergistic effect of love is portrayed by this card. The lovers together, are stronger than they are alone, and this makes it possible for them to achieve greater things together than individually.

The lovers card, apart from reminding us of the powerful effects of love, remind us of how important it is to work in conjunction with other people around us. In a world where everyone is trying so hard to be independent and adopting a 'mind-your-business' attitude, the lovers card serves to remind us that we can achieve so much more together than we can achieve working on our own.

The lovers card also portrays the divine property of love. Love is beautiful and can be an ecstatic feeling, but the true meaning of love is rooted in the love the divine has for us, His creations. Even true love that exists between two individuals cannot be properly established if the divine does not assent to it. So, the card serves to remind us of how a feeling as powerful as love should remind us of the powerful connection we share with the divine, and how He can make our lives so much more beautiful, if only we choose to accept Him.

The Lovers card is also about making choices. As we go through life as individuals, we are bound to find ourselves in circumstances where we have to make choices, some of which may be tough at times. The lovers make a choice to pursue happiness together, despite all odds. The card therefore implores us to seek out choices that guarantee our long-term happiness, and the long-term happiness of the people around us.

The Lovers card also reminds us to follow our hearts in our undertakings. Too often in life, we find ourselves carrying out other people's wishes instead of living our lives as we please. While it may be necessary to curtail some of our instincts, follow necessary instructions, and curb our own excesses, it is also extremely critical for us to follow our hearts as we go through life, and pursue our own passions and dreams. In the end, what an individual will remember is not how perfectly he managed to carry out other people's orders and create other people's dreams. What he will remember is how much he did or did not pursue his innermost desires.

In the image on the Lovers card of the RWS Tarot deck, there is a man and a woman, and the humans are looking up to an angel. This representation signifies the power of opposites, and how opposites can actually come together to produce stupendous results. This interpretation means that while differences would always exist between us as individuals, it is possible for us to choose to overlook those differences and make the decision to work together to achieve our common goals. As a matter of fact, it is possible for us as individuals to find strength in our differences, and channel those strengths to help us produce even better and more spectacular results.

The image of the two naked humans and the angel above also signifies the important of making the decision to either succumb to temptation or remain obedient to the commandments of the divine. As has been reiterated severally, the Lovers card is all about the choices we make – the choice to love someone despite their flaws, the choice to choose to work together with other people despite salient differences between ourselves and these people.

Another choice the Lovers card says we might have to make is the choice of either choosing to follow the straight, narrow and righteous path, or succumbing to the temptations of the world. As humans we always have the freewill to make our decisions and make our personal choices. but when we do that, it is important to put things into perspective. The fact is all actions eventually have consequences, and our choices are going to determine the rewards or punishments we would eventually reap.

The Lovers card also shows the shining sun – a representation of the consuming beauty of love, and its divine implications. Love has been described by many as the most beautiful feeling in the world, and it is because love is a choice; a choice to put another person's needs and feelings before yours, a choice to look out for the person you choose; to protect them and care for them despite all odds. The beauty of love comes from the personal sacrifices and the spirit of service that comes with it.

INTRINSIC CARD MEANING: The Lover's card can be said to have one central theme: making the right choices.

VII – THE CHARIOT

The chariot represents constant movement. The chariot serves to remind us, as querents, that in life, we must always strive to keep moving forward despite impediments in our way. It doesn't matter how pure your intentions are, or how strong your ambition is, there will always be challenges in your path that will threaten to not only stop you in your tracks, but also attempt to bring you to your knees and keep you there if you let them.

Therefore, the chariot represents the conscious decision to keep moving forward, whether it is racing forward at the speed of lightning, or crawling at a snail's pace in some instances. The important thing is to keep moving forward, no matter what.

As portrayed by the two beasts in the image driving the chariot forward and moving in opposite directions, sometimes, the problems that stand in the way of our progress are not external they are internal. Sometimes, to keep moving forward we need to resolve our internal conflicts and come to terms with who we really are first.

If you are not at peace with yourself, the internal war you will keep fighting constantly will sap you of the energy you were supposed to harness in moving forward. Therefore, to move forward, you must first prepare yourself on the inside to keep moving. It is when your internal resolve is rock solid that you would then be able to overcome external impediments.

In the Chariot card, the chariot is represented to be moving away from a city or a civilization of some sorts. This serves to remind us as individuals that sometimes, on the oath to success, we might have to leave comfort and convenience behind to face challenges and uncertainty. However, without these challenges we would face in the oath to success, we would never truly discover our capabilities, and we would never be able to efficiently manage the success that we seek when it comes. So this portrayal shows that while striving towards the realization of our dreams as individuals, it is extremely important to keep in mind that we will have to make important personal sacrifices.

Every inch that the chariot moves during its journey requires energy. This implies the journey to self-discovery and the actualization of the querent's dream is going to require him to put in the work every step of the way. No free passes. The struggle to keep going remains constant, and the querent needs to be mentally prepared that there is going it be a constant pressure on him by the feeble part of his mind to give up. So even after overcoming the normal reluctance to begin something big, he still needs to constantly suppress the urge to give up while battling any obstacles that may stand between him and his desired destination.

Finally, in the charioteer's hand, there is a wand. This wand represents the place of sheer will and determination in the movement of an individual towards his dreams. As movement proceeds, thigs might be quite tough at the start, but as the individual gains momentum by pressing forward, he becomes more confident about his abilities and gains the ability to keep moving even in the face of seemingly insurmountable challenges. Will and a firm resolve to keep moving help the individual to overcome all obstacles in his path to success.

In the card, the charioteer isn't holding any reins to control the chariot, and the sphinxes are opposing each other instead of working together towards the achievement of a common goal – moving forward.

The opposing sphinxes remind us that sometimes, the main cause of us not moving forward towards our goal is a riddle, just like the sphinxes are the universal symbols for riddles. The sphinxes are refusing to work together, thereby hampering the smooth movement of the chariot. Since the sphinxes themselves are symbols of riddles, it is highly pertinent for the charioteer (in this case, the querent) to first of all figure out the riddle, or the root cause of the delay in the movement before attempting to keep moving forward. Any attempt to progress without actually fixing the underlying problem will only cause further problems in the long run.

Finally, the crown and canopy of stars on the charioteer's head and on top of the chariot represent the importance of celestial direction and guidance in the movement of an individual towards his goals. The divine has an extremely critical role to play in ensuring that an individual begins to move towards his goals, and still keeps moving when the going gets tough.

INTRINSIC CARD MEANING: This card shows that the querent must keep moving, or start moving towards his goals, if he hasn't. The card also shows the victory of will and the desire to conquer even in the presence of intense difficulties.

VIII – STRENGTH

The strength card shows a lion, fierce and ruthless, being calmed by a gentle, calm-looking woman. Even at a glance, this card sends a very deep and important message – true strength doesn't always lie in force or violence, it most times lies in our ability to influence other people, to control their decisions, and to control our own emotions when we are pushed to the edge. The lion as an animal is assertive, aggressive, and always tends to go for the jugular when it hunts. The lion, however, for all its fierceness and power can be known to lack control and decorum, and that is where its weakness lies.

True strength lies in a different kind of power – the kind that the female in the image is exerting on the beast, calming it and controlling it, and coaxing it to abide by her own rules and wishes. The Strength card serves to remind us true strength does not come from inspiring fear in others. Even if fear manages to make you look powerful as an individual, its effect can only be fleeting, never permanent. This is because when people are ruled with fear, eventually when they are presented with an option that involves calmness and peace, they will go for that. And even if they don't, they are not likely to remain your meek slaves for long. Eventually, they will revolt, and you will lose your power.

The gentle hand of the female n the lion represents peace and tranquility. A truly strong person is not the one who is great at inspiring fear, but who is good at bringing peace and calmness to even the most violent of situations. So, to be truly strong, you need to help people to be able to find peace, not take away their peace.

The female figure calming the beast also represents the incredible power of femininity, and how the divine has bestowed females with the tender ability to calm and nurture even the wildest of beasts. The strength of the female is not physical, it is emotional. It is the ability to subtly overwhelm a beast's violent tendencies and persuade it to remain calm. The female's ability to take away the rashness and bloodlust of a beast represents the incredible power that the female gender has been bestowed with.

The image on the Strength card shows the connection between gentleness and divine power. The power of the divine can be tremendously devastating, but it is mostly calm, peaceful and forgiving. The female in this image represents the calming power of the divine even in the scariest of circumstances. The divine can always bring a man peace and tranquility if he truly seeks it.

The white gown represents the purity of the female's intentions. She has not come to deceive or betray the lion's trust; she has come to help it heal from the violence that is tearing it apart from the inside. She has come to truly provide succor, and to help the beast find lasting peace.

Finally, the lion's widely opened mouth, signifying a roar shows that even in the most daunting of circumstances, peace and calmness trump violence and fear. Fear may be temporarily powerful, but its effects withers over time. Only true peace actually lasts.

INTRINISIC CARD MEANING: True strength does not lie in violence, inspiring fear and conquering by force. True strength lies in the ability to subdue our own inappropriate tendencies and those of others with love and patience.

IX – THE HERMIT

The hermit card features a blue background, representing calmness, tranquility and peace, like the sky or a calm sea. Standing against the backdrop of the blue background is a mysterious cloaked figure holding a staff and a lantern, giving off an aura of a wizened, experienced and peaceful old man. Hermits are naturally reclusive, and are usually not obsessed with worldly possessions. They, instead, prefer to live extremely minimalistic lives, having only a few clothes, food and simple homes. They usually live in solitude, and may move very often in search of knowledge, wisdom and inner peace. The life of a hermit as a concept reminds us that we can never truly discover ourselves until we stop trying so hard to acquire every single worldly desire that we want.

Hermits have discovered the truth about the human existence – the more you have, the more you want. We all tend to get caught up in this vicious cycle, thinking that at some point, we would actually figure out a way to be happy and contented with what we have, but that time just never comes. Therefore, the hermit's main message is for us to take a step back, examine our lives, and actually determine if all the happiness, family ties and little, but significant moments that we sacrifice all the time in the pursuit of our worldly desires are actually worth it.

The hermit in the Hermit Card carries a lantern. The lantern emits a beam of light just bright enough for the hermit to find his way. The lantern represents a guiding light that aids the hermit along his path to finding himself, and discovering inner peace. The lantern represents more than just a conventional source of light. It represents the divine guidance that we as individuals get when we make the conscious decision to stop being overly materialistic or distracted by worldly desires and actually focus on making our stay and journey in this world an impactful one.

Dedicating your life to more than just worldly possessions helps you to discover yourself in ways you could never previously imagine. Your eyes gradually become clear to see that the path to happiness is not by accumulating a lot of worldly desires, it is by living a purposeful, impactful life.

The main point of the hermit card is self-discovery, finding the light that guides your way, and helping others to find their purpose and meaning in this world. The hermit lives a solitary life. Unlike the hierophant, his sole purpose is not to direct people towards paths of righteous living and walking in the faith. His sole purpose is to use his guiding light to find his path, and live his life to the best of his ability.

The hermit is more of a stellar example than a teacher. He goes on his solitary journey, and helps people who desire his help, because he has found out that helping others is the best way to find true bliss. So, the hermit's life is more of an example to be emulated, not a public classroom where everyone is taught or guided.

In the Universal Waite Deck, the hermit card shows a wise old man holding a lantern. Of course, this figure represents the hermit, and the lantern represents the divine light that guides his path as he progresses on his journey to inner peace and self-discovery. The lantern highlights the importance of a form of supernatural guidance as we try to forge our paths in the world.

Without some sort of light guiding our path, it becomes incredibly difficult to find our way, and then we tend to get lost, never really finding our purpose nor making impact. However, the lantern doesn't just fall into your lap, it has to be sought. To find your path to making impact in the world, you have to go back to the basics and seek guidance from the divine. After getting the divine light, it is now your job to keep going along the path it directs you to follow as you journey in pursuit of self-discovery.

In the hermit's hand is large staff that most experts interpret to be a rather large wand – indicating the importance of will and determination in the journey of the hermit. Just because you have found the guiding light, just because you have finally embarked upon your journey to self-discovery doesn't mean finding your purpose is going to be a walk in the park.

Just like in every journey in life, the journey to leading a purposeful life that doesn't just benefit you, but helps to make the world a better place is going to have serious challenges – discouragements from other people, the incessant temptation to give up, the hard decisions to give up your former frivolous and haphazard lifestyle – all these will take a sheer amount of will, courage and determination.

For you make any progress in your journey to self-discovery therefore, your resolve must be unshaken and unbreakable. Just like a strong staff supports a hermit and keeps him going when the journey gets hard and he gets weak, an unbreakable resolve to live a truly impactful life will keep you going as you journey towards self-discovery and a life dedicated not just to yourself, but to the betterment of the world.

INTRINSIC CARD MEANING: Finding purpose in life, the truth about your existence and living to make impact is going to require you to withdraw from worldly distractions to figure out your path.

X – THE WHEEL OF FORTUNE

The main concept behind the wheel is change; movement. In life, perhaps the most certain thing to happen between birth and death is change. Even if a person decides to not to get an education to actually ensure mental advancement, the individual still changes physically until he grows old and dies. As the wheel moves over a surface, at a particular point in time, a specific portion of the wheel is found at the top, while another is at the bottom, grinding against the dust.

However, soon enough, the one previously at the bottom comes on top, and the one on top is found at the bottom as the wheel keeps spinning to keep the vehicle going. The wheel is a perfect representation of life. Life never stops; not for a moment. Whether we, as individuals decide to keep fighting to make the best of our existence solely depends on us.

Of course, there are times when we tend to fall of the wagon, lose focus or lose the energy and drive to keep pushing on towards our dreams, but the wheel reminds us that life keeps going on, whether we choose to go on along with it, or we choose to remain stagnant at one spot, wallowing in self-pity. The continuous, unstopping tick-tock of the clock reminds you that with or without you, life is going to keep going on, and it reminds you, like life, to always keep moving.

Of course, you won't have the energy to always be on the move. Sometimes, life gets hard, sometimes life breaks us. However, when life rips us apart and threatens to keep us stagnant, it is our job to remember that life is not stopping, and neither should we. We should pick ourselves back up, and keep moving. Change is constant, we must continuously evolve.

Just as the wheel spins evenly, making each part of the wheel pass through a particular position during one revolution, so does life spin. While life's spins may not be completely even; some people suffer more than they live well, while it is the other way round for some people. However, the important thing to note is life does spin. Today might be extremely fabulous for you, but you need to realize that the wheel of your life is only spinning through the good times at the moment. Whether you like it or not; whether you choose to admit it or not, the tough times are going to arrive, and it would be in your best interest for these times to meet you prepared.

Just like the common wheel of fortune can stop unpredictably at any point, so can life! Life can choose to hand you any kind of fortune after a spin; it might be good; it might be bad. But the important thing is that the wheel of fortune always stops pointing to something, and it mostly stops abruptly. So, life can hand you any type of fortune. It might be fabulously wonderful, or it may be depressingly saddening. It is, however, your duty as a strong individual to make the best of whatever life's wheel of fortune hands to you.

The Wheel of Fortune card also serves to remind us of the uncertainty of life. Nothing is guaranteed; nothing is promised. Life is dynamic, ever changing. Today, you might be rich, the next day you might be dirt poor. As the wheel of life is spun and we look at the wheel longingly hoping for the best, we can only wait with bated breath and see how the wheel turns out.

Of course, by the dint of hard work and dedication, we can make spirited efforts to create better lives for ourselves and our loved ones, but the wheel of fortune still serves to remind us that life still remains a game of chance, a wheel of fortune where nothing is promised, and uncertainty reigns supreme. You can work extremely hard and still end up unsuccessful. You can work very hard, and with luck on your side, end up incredibly wealthy and influential. It's all about where the wheel eventually ends up.

In the Universal Waite Card, there is a sphinx at the top of the wheel, representing the mystery that life is. Life is a complex riddle, and it is not decipherable from the start. Nobody can give a hint of what the wheel of fortune's final declaration would be. It's only after the wheel stops spinning that we can actually say for sure exactly what life has had in store for us all along. So, while change is guaranteed, the result of the change is unpredictable.

The figures in the four corners of the card represent the four main zodiac signs, which are interpreted in this context as the foundations of the world. The world is built on change, and as the wheel spins, different parts come in contact with different signs during the course of the revolution. The zodiac signs remind us that as change progresses, we tend to pass through various phases before arriving at our final destination.

Therefore, if we are stuck at a point at the moment, it is imperative for us to remember that this is just a season, and it will pass. If things are being rosy, it is still important for us to remember the wheel is still spinning. In actual reality, the wheel keeps spinning; we continue to experience change and evolution as humans until death comes knocking. That is when the wheel finally stops turning.

INTRINSIC CARD MEANING: The Wheel of Fortune card simply symbolizes the importance of change in our lives. If a querent asks a question and this card comes up, it signifies an extremely significant alteration in the status quo is about to happen.

XI – JUSTICE

The card of justice talks about the consequences of the actions we carry out as humans. Even though, to the naïve mind, life may seem like a random sequence of occurrences, the truth is that sooner or later, people eventually reap the consequences of their actions. People tend to go through life with the mindset they will just have to give in life what it would take to ensure they are successful. In their wild pursuit of wealth and success, they gag their conscience and tow the path of immorality, violence and cheating just to achieve their goals. Sometimes, people like this achieve their goals, and other times, they don't. However, what always holds true is that they eventually pay for their crimes.

However, justice is not all about bad people, it's about good people too. A lot of people work extremely hard, or do good deeds in secret, trying their best to make the world a better place. Justice would find this category of people, and they would be paid in their own coin. Life may not have a strict pattern to it, and it may all seem haphazard from the outside, but as we keep going, we find out whether we like it or not, we eventually reap the seeds that we sow.

The Justice sits between two pillars, representing a threshold between one place and another. The justice at the threshold ushers in good people who have dedicated themselves to making a positive impact on the world into a place of bliss, tranquility and true peace. The justice serves as the fair gatekeeper, who grants people entry based on their deeds. Where you go now directly depends on exactly what you have done in the past.

On the other hand, of course, people who have dedicated their lives to cheating people and trampling on other people's rights just because they have the power to do so, will eventually face inevitable ruin when the time for reckoning comes. The justice is calm, unfazed and unruffled. Justice will not be bribed, compromised or manipulated. The Justice card represents the purest form of reliability – nothing is going to change his decision, and his decision is solely based on the truth.

Beyond the threshold, an individual is ushered into a realm of true understanding. After experiencing first-hand, the powers of justice, and how there is actually order in this seemingly disorganized world after all, the individual, whether he has been rewarded or punished for his past deeds comes to understand how life truly has a way of paying back people for what they do. People who do the same thing may not be paid back in the same exact way, but somehow, eventually, every single person gains a fair reward for their actions.

In the Universal Waite Card, the Justice sits before the veil, showing that he is custodian of the threshold. He is the one who determines who steps through, where each individual goes, and when the time of reckoning of each individual is due. Some people live extremely frivolous lives funded by the proceeds of crime, corruption and mismanagement.

However, just because it is not time for justice to come calling, they actually believe that there is no consequence to their actions. In the long run, however, they discover, to their dismay that justice really does exist, but then, it would be too late for them to amend their ways. The veil also indicates secrecy and mystery; the wisdom of the justice may go beyond human comprehension. How the justice uses intricate logic to judge who deserves what is sometimes a mystery.

Some people who have committed extremely heinous crimes in secret would think they can go scot-free because their crimes went undiscovered. Justice, however, manages to comes for us all, uncovering even the deepest and darkest secrets and mysteries.

The Justice is also seen to don a crown. This symbolizes authority and command. Whatever the justice says is final. He has the supreme ability to reward and to condemn based on the facts and the truth at his disposal, and nothing a condemned person says or does will ever change the fact that he will get the judgement he deserves. The authority of the justice means that nobody can render his pronouncements invalid; he is supreme and infallible. Justice does not make mistakes, neither does it intentionally do criminals favors, or punish the righteous. The justice passes judgements with fairness, and he will not be overpowered or overthrown.

The sword and scales in the card represent the power to punish and the fairness of the justice. The Justice holds the supreme power to make immoral people pay for their misdeeds, but before he punishes them, he gives them a fair trial using the scales. The scales are used to examine the facts, and where it is evident that an individual's bad deeds outweigh the good, then such a person is doomed.

Unlike the conventional feminine symbol of justice, the figure representing justice in the Major Arcana suit is not blindfolded. While being blindfolded might be interpreted as impartiality, the Justice can actually see the facts, examine them critically, and make wise pronouncements to ensure that the guilty doesn't go unpunished.

INTRINSIC CARD MEANING: The Justice card, when pulled, simply means a querent is soon going to be facing the consequences of past actions.

XII – THE HANGED MAN

In earlier explanations of this card, older experts used to believe that the hanged man represents a traitor who is now being punished for his misdeeds, hence being hanged upside-down to serve as a deterrent to others. However, in recent explanations, the Hanged man is now seen as a symbol of quiet acceptance, an individual who has come to terms with his current situation, and is done struggling against the inevitable.

In life, sometimes, it is difficult coming to terms with prevailing situations, and just accepting our fates. Most times, we are told to always fight to the death for what we want, and if we feel we do not deserve what are getting, we should make all efforts to ensure that we get exactly what it is that we want and deserve. However, sometimes, in life we find ourselves in situations that we are truly helpless against. In these situations, struggling is useless; whatever will happen is still going to happen.

Therefore, like the hangman, in these situations, instead of expending our energy, resources, time, and even sacrificing valuable relationships just to prove specific points or get a particular desire, it is preferable for us to be tranquil and calm, and just follow the proceedings. In these situations, we must always remind ourselves that circumstances in life are only transient and bound to change. When we have this mindset, we would be able to find the inner peace we need to come to terms with the situation, and weather the storm with calmness and stability.

Surrendering, at times may be harder than keeping up the struggle. It might be because of an individual's ego, because of the resources he has lost to the fight, because of the people he has lost, or because of other kinds of sacrifices he has made. Whatever he has had to give up to keep the fight going makes it very difficult to surrender, because he has truly lost a lot.

However, the only way that individual is going to actually find peace and prevent further destruction to himself is to simply surrender, stay calm, and weather the storm in silence. When we let go of trying to be in control of bad situations that we have no way of stopping, we will find ourselves attaining incredible levels of inner peace and personal satisfaction. Things we cannot change will not faze us anymore – we just let them slide.

In the Universal Waite Card, there is a halo around the hanged man's head. This is interpreted to mean spiritual, divine understanding that comes from deep reflection and the conscious decision to stop struggling against the inevitable. When we let go of circumstances we have no control over, we leave the fight for the divine to fight for us, while trusting and believing that eventually we would be alright. Reaching this stage of enlightenment helps us to find true peace and happiness even in the midst of our troubles. Finding calmness and hope even in the presence of such a great tribulation as being hanged upside down can only mean one thing – an individual has found spiritual guidance.

In the card also, the hanged man is hung from a living tree. This is interpreted to mean that the hanged man's tribulations have helped him to further deepen his relationship with the divine, as the living tree represents the power of the supernatural. So, instead of allowing his troubles to break down, he instead finds strength from the fact he knows that the divine has him covered, and he is going to be alright.

The tree being rooted to earth also represents the practicality of the hang man's surrender. His decision is grounded in practicality. He has weighed all his options and figured out that the best thing to do in his situation is to simply surrender to his troubles and find peace even in the middle of his tribulations. The practicality of his decision clears off all his worries, because he is assured he has taken the most logical decision, considering his current circumstances.

INTRINSIC CARD MEANING: The hangman represents the concept of surrendering to a situation voluntarily while hoping for the best, instead of letting it wear you out and still eventually conquer you.

XIII – DEATH

When people hear of death, a feeling of dread and trepidation tends to overwhelm them. When death takes away loved ones, we grieve and hurt because our relationship with the dead person has been rudely cut short. All we have left of the person is memories, and we are unsure of what becomes of the person that's gone. However, death is not all about the end of a phase, it is also the opportunity for the beginning of another. While death may symbolize the end of an individual's stay in the physical world, it is the only gateway through which the human soul can transcend the barriers of the physical to enter the world of the supernatural.

Therefore, death is also about transformations and new beginnings, and sometimes, even the promise of a better existence. However, for the new existence to begin, the pain of death must first be felt. The end may be painful and devastating, but it has to occur before the new era can begin. Despite the fact that people desire the new beginnings that come after death, most people find it very difficult to bear the pain that comes with the ending of life as we know it.

The concept of death and transition is one that holds true in our lives here on earth. For us to actually move from where we are to where we want to be, it means we must first lose what we have. We must learn to let go of what we have for what we desire, and that is a difficult thing to even consider. Leaving certainty, security and comfort for the uncertain can be downright scary and intimidating, but it is a price we have to pay for the progress we desire.

The death card, and the concept of death in itself also symbolizes the importance of grief and pain in making us stronger and capable of handling the success that we actually desire. When people die, we grieve. The pain usually seems unbearable at first, and the enormity of the pain makes us feel like dying too. However, as we struggle with the hurt and devastation, we become stronger and more powerful, and when we finally emerge from the depths of bereavement, we emerge unstoppable, tough and stoic. The pain has driven us into the ground, but against all odds, we have found our way out, and we have emerged only stronger and more determined to win.

Therefore, in life, loss is necessary for new and better things to be discovered. Losing puts you through pain and anguish that refines you, filters out your weaknesses and consolidates your strengths, so when you eventually emerge victorious, you are actually able to handle the success you have achieved through pure pain and struggle.

In the Universal Waite Card, different approaches to handling the pain and loss that comes with death are illustrated. The fainting king represent people who lose themselves temporarily to the pain. The begging bishop represents people who try frantically to change what has happened, even though it is unchangeable. The swooning maiden represents people who have the capacity to act, but remain transfixed and hope to be rescued. The innocent kid truly has no idea how to handle the pain, and struggles to find his way through the confusing maze of the pain.

The sunrise, the white rose and the phoenix represent the hope a better life after the end of a phase. This implies that death does not represent absolute finality, instead it just enables the cessation of an era so that another one can begin. The skulls, reapers and flames represent the pain of death which can be terribly devastating at first, but which eventually passes to make us stronger, more powerful and more self-reliant.

INTRINSIC CARD MEANING: The card represents death has a painful ending which helps to usher in the dawn of a new beginning.

XIV: TEMPERANCE

The concept of temperance is all about balance and moderation. However, in the real world, balance is not always about complete stark equality, instead it is about combining just the right amount of different components of life to ensure that a steady and stable overall balance is achieved. In life, equality is always emphasized, but the truth is that equality is not always the answer to the actual problems of the world. In concept, equality sounds fair – everybody gets the same thing, the same amount of time is dedicated to every single activity…but that almost never works. This is because in the real world, the solution to most problems we face is not equality, it is equity.

Equity doesn't state that everybody gets the same thing, it states that everybody gets the amount that is rightfully theirs to ensure a stable and sustainable society. Some people genuinely need more than others, just like some endeavors genuinely require more time, effort and attention than others. So if for the purpose of equality, you attempt to evenly distribute your time across all your activities – grooming, eating, working, sleeping…you will soon find out your life will begin to fall apart because you will be dedicating way too little time to the critical things that require major chunks of your time.

So, the point of temperance is keeping important issues in focus to ensure a steady balance in our lives. Not all things require all our attention and effort – we can't afford to do everything. We would only wear ourselves out. Temperance reminds us to concentrate on the critical aspects of our lives and carve out small periods of time regularly for less important endeavors.

Temperance reminds us that for an appreciable result to be achieved, the right components must be combined in the right proportions. That directly means some things would have to be done more than others for a great result to be achieved.

In the Universal Waite Card, there is an angel with one foot on land and one foot on water – this indicates the importance of balance that allows the magic to happen – the magic of water flowing between the cups, thereby defying gravity. Striking a perfect balance between the various aspects of our lives helps us to discover a new dimension of happiness, joy and contentment. We would continually find out that we achieve impressive results because we have taken the pain to ensure that all necessary requirements are put in place.

The halo in the image signifies serenity and divine peace. Achieving balance in your life will bring you true peace and tranquility. You won't have to be in a constant state of worry and jeopardy, unlike people whose lives are unbalanced. People who do not pay attention to balance would find themselves constantly stressed out because they would keep running from pillar to post trying to keep their lives steady. However, when you pay attention to balance from the start, you build upon the existing balanced foundation and find true peace of mind.

The red wings in the image signify the power that comes from temperance. The two wings are equally balanced, enabling flight. If one is shorter than the other or positioned lower below the other, the efficiency of flight is compromised. The wings show the incredible, yet subtle power in the concept of temperance.

INTRINSIC CARD MEANING: The temperance card teaches us to constantly keep different parts of our lives balanced to ensure long-term stability, security and progress.

XV – THE DEVIL

The devil, like death, is a frequently misunderstood entity. In the context of this card, the devil is not regarded as a supremely evil being who forces individuals into damnation. Instead, the devil is regarded as a complex union of the concepts of the Lovers and the Hierophant. The Lovers portray the principle of choice, and the willingness to bear the consequences of choices made., through the bitter and through the joyful. The Hierophant on the other hand, represents the principle of leadership through action. The devil brings together the principles of choice and leadership by example. The devil card is all about making a choice to follow a path that leads to destruction.

The devil has a flashy exterior, an attractive and tempting trap that is used to lure greedy people in. However, the devil does not force. The devil is all about making choices. The devil gives you convincing reasons to follow his path, and then leaves you to make your own choices. If you now allow yourself to be confused by the devil's antics to the extent you end up falling into his trap, then that is totally your own doing, not the devil's. The devil only presents you with a choice.

Where the hierophant urges individuals to walk in faith and live lives worthy of emulation, the devil urges individuals to follow their most destructive and evil instincts without batting an eyelid. The devil represents an epitome of wrong choices which eventually leads to self-imposed bondage and addiction. People tend to make choices based on what's on the outside without fully taking their time to investigate the nature of the choices that they are making. After making these choices, they find themselves disappointed, or even worse, trapped by their own choices.

They are thereafter forced to live with the consequences of their wrong choices, because more often than not, wrong choices may be extremely difficult to reverse. In extreme cases, people lured into evil lives may eventually find themselves fascinated with the allure of the darkness and actually get addicted to leading destructive lives which eventually leads them to damnation. The consequences of the choices of the people who make wrong choices based on temptation is they tend to get held back from making progress in most of the key aspects of their lives.

In the Universal Waite Card, the stereotypical image of the devil is shown with the curved horns, representing the concept of evil. This simply implies that when people make wrong choices based on tempting exteriors, they usually end up finding themselves in extremely dark and dangerous circumstances they are usually not capable of wriggling themselves out of. Just below the devil in the cards, male and female figures with tails and horns are depicted, making a mockery of humanity, and showing how we can become slaves to the consequences of our own wrong choices. Wrong choices usually have far-reaching effects people do not usually immediately consider before making them due to the desire of the human nature for instant gratification.

The loose chains around the feet of the human figures shows that there is actually a slim possibility of escape if an individual is truly committed to amending his ways. However, the enslavement and bondage of these people is more mental than physical. They are not being forced by the devil to stay, instead, they have sunk so deep into the pit of evil and wrongdoing that finding their way back to morality and righteous living becomes almost impossible.

INTRINSIC CARD MEANING: The Devil represents the wrong choices we make that become detrimental to our long-term progress.

XVI – THE TOWER

Towers are often regarded as symbols of strength, endurance, stability and pride. However, for towers to be constructed, whatever was on that piece of land has to be removed or demolished first. Now, the structure that had to be torn down for the tower to rise might have been a cherished structure; it might have been a home that ensconced a lot of memories of happy times. However, for the tower, an even more powerful structure, to be erected, the structure had to fall first.

The Tower card reminds us that when it is time to move forward in life onto bigger and greater things, it is important to first of all give up things that might hold us back first. Now what may be holding you back from progressing onto bigger things as a person might not be as serious as a building, it might be a habit or a person. Whatever it is holding you back, you have to let it go so you can spring forth and actually live up to your potentials.

When the former structure that existed before the tower was brought down, a lot of people would have been wondering why the homeowner was deliberately tearing down what might have been a seemingly perfect building. But the owner knew what he had in mind. He knew, deep inside that he desired something even better than what he had currently, and he knew that for his dreams to come true, he had to make uncomfortable sacrifices that other people saw as illogical.

The tower is then built using the ruins of the old building in combination with new materials. The old structure did not only give space for the construction of the tower, it also served as a source for some of the materials used in building the new, stronger structure. This serves to remind us it is only when we completely give up things standing in the way of your progress that we can actually begin our journey to achieving stupendous success.

In the Universal Waite Card, the tower is being struck severely by lightning, but despite the forces of the storm against it, it stands tall, proud and strong, and doesn't falter. In life, we need to be able to weather the regular small storms and the occasional devastating ones. However, to actually weather our storms, we need to build ourselves to be strong and indestructible like the tower. A tower is not built in a rush; a rushed tower soon comes crashing down, rendering all the rushed efforts put into building it useless, and possibly even destroying other structures around it.

A solid personality is not built in a day, either. It takes time, training and determination, but with endurance, an individual gets to that point where he has built himself to be a tower of strength that no storm can collapse.

The image in the card also shows humans falling from the tower in the storm. This has been interpreted to show the need for falling and new beginnings. To achieve remarkable success in life, sometimes we have to fall from the positions of power that we hold and are proud of. However, if we truly have bigger dreams, it is likely that we may have to fall from our positions in the tower to start from the very basics again.

Starting from the basics means the things that used to hold us back – the feeling of being the comfort zone, the fear of losing what we already have - are not there again. We have lost everything, but we have also been given an incredible chance, the opportunity to try again afresh with no limitations whatsoever.

INTRINSIC CARD MEANING: The tower card is interpreted to mean an unexpected change that may be seen to be detrimental at first, but that actually leads to bigger and more remarkable success than what was lost.

XVII – THE STAR

The star is generally regarded as a symbol of astonishing brilliance, beauty and power. The Star card symbolizes hope shining through in dark times just like the stars illuminate the dark night. A lot of times, we find it very difficult, while in the middle of tribulations to stay strong on our own. The star serves to remind us of the possibility of finding hope and light even in the darkest places.

The star also reminds us that it doesn't matter what's going on in our surroundings, we owe it to ourselves, and to the people who look up to us to be a beacon of hope and brilliance. It doesn't matter how dark the night sky is, it doesn't matter whether the moon is full, halved or absent, the stars continue shine with the best of their abilities, lighting up the night sky with their magical glows. Therefore, the star card reminds us to try out best to shine brilliantly regardless of our situations, and to never let depressing circumstances weigh us down. Come rain, come sunshine, we must always strive to bless the world with the amazing brilliance of our glow.

The star card also represents the powerful combination of the soft and gentle, yet amazingly powerful qualities of the lights shined by stars. Even though starlight is cool and placid, it is fiercely piercing, and reaches down over millions of kilometers to the earth. The starlight is symbolic of the power that lies in gentility and calmness. Empty vessels tend to make the loudest noises, and it is the still waters that actually run deepest.

The stars remind us never to forget the power in serenity and keeping calm even when everyone around us is losing themselves to the chaos. It is our responsibility to recognize the power in being cool, calm and collected even in the middle of madness, because it is only with our placidity that we can help to restore the order that has been lost. Starlight, therefore, brilliantly illustrates the relationship between calmness and enduring strength.

The light of the stars also serves to remind us of the hope of refreshment and rejuvenation even after trouble and tribulation. The sun shines brilliantly through the day, and then sets, leaving darkness in its wake. However, the stars come as a symbol of hope, that all light is not truly lost, and that even though the sun is temporarily gone, we would still have a different, yet beautiful form of light to gaze upon. As individuals, the star card communicates to us, the message of restored faith and renewed purpose. Even though the daylight has gone, and darkness has replaced it, the stars remind us to always endeavor to find the light in the darkness; the hope in the despair.

It is only when we choose to look for the great sides of even the worst situations that we would truly discover true happiness and peace of mind. Therefore, instead of concentrating on the bad or the trouble surrounding us (the darkness), we are instead encouraged to look for the stars, appreciate them, and utilize them to the best of our ability until the sun shines again.

In the Universal Waite Card, there is naked figure indicating vulnerability. This communicates the message that in the dark times, we are more susceptible to harm and losing our way, straying off our paths. However, if we choose not to focus on the darkness, but on the light of the stars that accompany it, we may find out that we can still find hope even in the darkness, and find our way through till the sun comes out again.

The water being poured from the twin pitchers are interpreted as the twin concepts of faith and trust. To be able to see the hope being radiated by the stars and derive comfort and succor from the gentle light of the stars, we must have faith and trust that the stars will help us, despite their small size, and we must trust that the darkness is only temporary, because sunrise is not too far away.

Faith and trust are two important components of the universe's divine flow that we as humans must never lose grasp of. We must always hold on to our faith and trust ourselves and the divine that only the good things are going to happen to us. It is even more critical than ever to keep hope and faith alive during the dark times, because it is these twin concepts that will keep us going through the darkness until the sun rises for us again.

INTRINSIC MEANING OF THE CARD: The Star card communicates the message of divine guidance, serenity and the promise of hope even in the darkest of times.

XVIII – THE MOON

The moon has been renowned for centuries as a symbol of feminine energy and power, and of course a hallmark of change. Just like life, the moon is ever-changing, in its shape, it's brightness and its brilliance. On some days, it is not even visible at all, on some days it is so dim that it is easy to forget that it is there, and on some days, it is so stunningly brilliant that it lights up every single thing its light touches with a magical glow. The moon reminds us that life is all about changing seasons – today may be incredibly bright, tomorrow may be dim – our lives are all subject to change.

The Moon Card reminds us to take all forms of change we encounter in good faith and enjoy every aspect of the journey of life. Just as change is a natural property if the moon, it is also a natural property of life. Whether we want it to happen or not, life is going to change and it is up to us as individuals to be ready for, and of course make the best use of life's constant changes.

The moon is a shadowy celestial figure. It shines bright in the night, but unlike the sun that lights up the sky and exposes everything on the surface of the earth to the scrutiny of the eye, the moon is a different kind of entity. Even though it illuminates, it also conceals. No matter how bright the moon is, it is still hard to spot some things under its glow, and its light may even help to mask the true nature of things. This property of the moon makes it a perfect means of masking the true identity of particular things.

This property of the moon serves to remind us that things are not always as they seem, and it doesn't make a lot of sense to jump into hasty conclusions. When faced with confusing circumstances, instead of just drawing hasty conclusions, the moon card reminds us to take our time to make in-depth investigations to find out the actual truth before taking any rash actions.

The moon has also been known to heighten intuition and boost creativity in so many fields of human endeavor. The beauty of the moon and its intrinsic mystery remind us that so much inspiration and creativity can be derived from even seemingly insignificant everyday things, if only we choose to ponder deeply over the beauty and significance of these entities. The moon for instance is always present, but if we are in our element and choose to ponder about the complex nature of the moon and its commanding beauty, we might find ourselves getting even more curious and inquisitive about its nature, and we may find ourselves inspired to go on to accomplish great things just because of the inspiration that the moon has given us.

Just as it heightens creativity and intuition however, so does the moon also foster fear and delusions. Despite the moon's light being superbly bright, it still does not change the fact that our world is in darkness, and with the darkness comes the fear of the unknown and the unseen. In the darkness, it is easy to hallucinate and see things that are not there. The moon card, therefore, reminds us to be extremely careful and cautious while in confusing circumstances to avoid making tragic mistakes or falling into deadly traps.

In the Universal Waite Card, the moon is seeing to be shining over a crayfish, representing the deep fears that come with being the dark – the fear of falling, the fear of being taken, the fear of losing our way and getting lost forever. When the problems of life come knocking and we feel desolate, lonely, and alone, we must always remember that our fears are characteristic of an individual being in the dark. We must, therefore, always keep in mind that darkness is just a temporary state of affairs, not the true representation of things. We must always keep in mind that the darkness will be lifted and good times will come again.

The wolf in the image represents the intense, serious and sometimes deadly responses that the moon can elicit. Wolves are known to howl at full moons. A full moon sends a powerful light from the dark which penetrates the darkness. The creatures if the darkness on sighting this light will definitely response to the presence of the light. When in the darkness, therefore, whether you are the individual serving as the moon, beaming your light through to help others find their way, or you are the individual trying to find your way through the darkness using the light beamed by an entity representing the moon, you must always keep in mind that the moon elicits intense responses from the darkness, hence you need to always keep your guard up.

The towers represent a threshold that can be interpreted as a gateway into the new phase of a journey – or of course, the break of a new day. The moon may endure through the night, but when darkness lifts, the moon goes away and the sun rises again. The threshold reminds us that the darkness is a part of the journey that must be complicated for the destination to be reached. Therefore, when we find ourselves trying desperately to find our way through the darkness, we should always remember that the darkness is only a part of the natural sequence of events that is bound to be over at one point or the other.

THE INRINSIC MEANING OF THE CARD: The Moon card represents the concepts of change, deception uncertainty, and revelations of secret truths. Nothing in life is guaranteed to remain constant, and when the moon shines, secrets hidden in the darkness are revealed. We must be careful, however, because in the presence of the moonlight, not everything is at it seems.

XIX – THE SUN

The sun, for centuries has always been regarded as a symbol of positivity – joy, pleasantness, bliss, ecstasy and delight. The sun lights up the world and shows its beauty.

The Sun card, therefore, represents happiness, positivity and delight. In life there are usually two types of bliss – one that is earned through strife, sacrifice and sometimes war. This is hard-earned peace that has come at a great cost. This is not what the sun stands for. The sun stands for gentle bliss and tranquility that comes as a gift – moments to treasure and hold dear. The sun card reminds us of those small happy moments in life that are usually unplanned and not worked for; that just fall into our laps and remain ingrained in our memories forever. To achieve major successes, sacrifices and intense work may be required, but in the kind of happiness the sun card represents, a gift of clarity, peace and tranquility is received.

In the Universal Waite Card, an image of a child riding a regal white is noticeable. This represents the innocent, child-like joy and delight that the Sun card represents – a joy that is pure, ecstatic and knows no pain or tribulation. The sun card represents the little joys of life for which major sacrifices are not made. It is these little joys that eventually last longest in our memories because they remind us of times filled with untainted joy.

The sunflowers in the picture also represent bliss and colorful delight –pure and natural in its beauty. The Sun card is all about natural peace, joy, beauty and clarity. The sunflowers portray the magnificence of a beautiful day – often overlooked, but when thought about, is actually spectacular.

INTRINSIC MEANING OF THE CARD: The sun card simply refers to peaceful clarity and joy.

XX – JUDGEMENT

While the Justice card emphasizes the importance of consequences of actions and inactions, the Judgement card represents something different – it represents response to a call. In most religions, the day of judgment is a day when all souls would be called forth; summoned to be judged. The judgement card tells the querent that it would soon be time to hearken to a particular call. Many times in life, we find ourselves hearing calls that we might or might not want to yield depending on the nature of the call, and of course, prevailing circumstances. The judgment card tells the querent in advance that a call that would have to be heeded is on its way, and the person should be on the lookout for a call that should not be ignored.

Calls, in this context come in many ways – opportunities for career progress, opportunities for education, meeting a new person and being offered the chance of a new relationship – the possibilities of what could constitute a call are practically endless. However, the most important thing to note is the querent should be on the lookout for opportunities, requests or commands that should be heeded and not ignored.

The Judgement card is also a representation of forgiveness – it reminds the querent of the importance of forgiveness. The need to forgive may even come as a call out to an individual through a wide variety of means. In life, forgiveness is one of the ways by which an individual can truly let go of a huge burden and find inner peace. Holding a grudge is like bearing a heavy burden – it doesn't hurt the person you have refused to forgive, but it definitely hurts you, and it kills you slowly from the inside, day in day out.

So, instead of hurting yourself and straining under the burden of the grudges and ill-feelings you have towards others, heed the call of forgiveness instead. Lay your heart bare and unconditionally forgive the people who have done wrong to you. Remind yourself that revenge would only bring temporary respite, that's if it brings any respite at all. The pain in your soul will still remain, and it will continue to haunt you. Therefore, to truly get rid of your pain once and for all, it is important for you to make a conscious decision to forgive those who have transgressed against you.

The Judgement card signifies a call, but it does not signify the outcome of the call that we are meant to heed. If we heed the call and carry out the responsibility required of us to the best of our ability, then bliss and satisfaction may arise. If the call is heeded, but the responsibility poorly carried out, the results may be discontentment and sadness. If the call is completely ignored, there may be dreadful consequences, and there may be no consequences at all. The point is the outcome of heeding or ignoring the call is not certain; the card only tells the querent about an important call that should be responded to will soon be heard.

In the Universal Waite Card, the image on the judgement card is reminiscent of a typical judgement day scene. As mentioned earlier, judgement day is not only about fairness and justice, it is also about summoning of souls. It is the response, voluntary or forced, of the souls to the call that leads to judgement being carried out. Therefore, the judgment card symbolizes a call to duty, to judgement or even to reward.

In the image on the judgement card, an angel is blowing a trumpet and souls are being liberated from their caskets. This represents the nature of calls that cannot be ignored and calls that lead to important events such as awakenings or fundamental paradigm shifts. While some calls may be inconsequential and heeding them may be optional, so may there be calls to a major transition that must be heeded for progress to occur or for a new phase of life to begin.

INTRINSIC CARD MEANING: The querent is warned of an impending call that needs to be responded to.

XXI – THE WORLD

The world card represents finishing or completing a phase of life and stepping out onto a new one. Its interpretation makes it perfect as the last card of the Major Arcana deck. Life is all about stages and phases, and whether we like it or not, we must go through every single step of each stage to achieve the progress and eventual success that we desire. Therefore, the world card signifies the end of a very major phase of life, and the beginning of a new age.

The world card is generally also interpreted to mean an incredible achievement that has been worked for over a long period is finally on the way. The World card doesn't represent a sudden blessing or a quick reward, it signifies the approach of a long-anticipated milestone in an individual's life.

According to experts in interpretation, the world is not just a symbol of joy and pride at completing a phase of life and making it out brilliantly, it is also a symbol of recognition, and appreciation. The individual is not only going to be happy for his success at reaching the end of a phase, he is also going to be recognized and celebrated for making it through to the end despite all the challenges that stood in his way. Arriving at the end of the phase being celebrated will open up new, powerful doors for him that would help him to have more influence to make the world a better place; hence the general celebration.

The World Card also represents the flow between endings and beginnings. This life is all about endings and beginnings, the end of one day is the beginning of another; the end of one phase is simply the beginning of another. Therefore, we must not get too conceited when we achieve long-awaited successes, because it only means we are about to a begin a new phase of our journey in the world, and there are many people who have passed through the gateway we are passing through too.

In all, the world card signifies everything is going click into place. All the sacrifices the querent has made just to make sure all his dreams come true will finally be worth it; the end is going to justify the means. The World card serves to also remind us, when the going gets tough to always keep the realization of our goals in focus. We must constantly remember why we started our journey in the first place, we must constantly remind ourselves of the change we hope to effect in the world with the achievement we are trying to acquire. We must never forget to let the importance of our goals motivate us to keep going through the tough times, because when the rewards are finally reaped, it will be all worth it.

In the image on the world card of the Universal Waite deck, there is a huge laurel wreath with a figure in the middle – this signifies honor, achievement and celebration. The querent is being told that very soon, he would get the recognition and respect he deserves for all the sacrifices he has been making towards achieving his goal. Also noticeable on the wreath in the form of lemniscates, are bright red ribbons. These ribbons symbolize the place of the divine in the achievement of success. The querent has come so far, and is now at the brink of achieving his age long goals, but he must be made to understand that he couldn't have surmounted all the obstacles he faced alone. The divine, understanding the nobility of his intentions had been by him every step of the way to enable him to achieve his goal and the divine is now ready to lead him on to the next stage of his life.

There are also four major zodiac signs in the image, indicating the importance of seasons in the existence of man. The time comes to begin – to sow a seed. The time also comes to strive to ensure a bountiful harvest; this is the time for sacrifices, for facing obstacles, for true, deep patience. Finally, the time comes for the harvest – for celebration and recognition of all the efforts that had been put in all along into making the success a reality.

INTRINSIC MEANING OF THE CARD: The world card simply informs the querent the end of a phase is at hand, and the dawn of a new beginning is not far off.

THE MINOR ARCANA

The cards of the Major Arcana were described as representations and predictions of major life-changing events, massive change, paradigm shifts, new phases of life and ends of existences. However, the cards of the Minor Arcana tend to represent less severe revelations, as they are usually predictions of minor, everyday events that are bound to happen as normal occurrences.

The cards of the Minor Arcana, therefore, do not represent any serious or life-changing events, they symbolize predictions that tend towards the mundane. The cards of the Minor Arcana, excluding the court cards are going to be reviewed in this section, and then the court cards would be independently examined in a following section.

As you go through the cards of the Minor Arcana, you can endeavor to compare their intrinsic meanings to mundane or slightly serious events that you have experienced in your life of late, and see how their interpretations relate to your experiences. Here we go.

ACE OF WANDS

The ace of wands is the first card in the 'Wands' suit of the Minor Arcana. As discussed earlier, the wands suit represents the fire element, symbolizing passion, energy and intensity related to an individual's career, a life journey or an important personal project. In any suit whatsoever, the ace usually represents a gift or an unexpected opportunity that soon passes. In life, we come across important opportunities that may have long-term benefits in our daily lives.

Some people realize the potential in these opportunities and take the time and effort to make the most of these opportunities, and end up reaping the long-term rewards. Other people squander the little, daily opportunities that come around once in a while, and then they complain about how their lives are not progressing or how they are not performing up to the standards of their colleagues.

The ace of wands, reminds us, in our daily lives, to be conscious of seemingly small opportunities, and not to squander the little chances we get. We must always be on the lookout for even the smallest chances that can help us grow to become better individuals, and of course have a significant impact on the world we live in.

The ace of wands is also an indication of great potential in an opportunity that is about to be encountered. Therefore, the querent is urged to not squander even the small-looking opportunities that come his way, as they might be the key to his success. The ace of wands is generally regarded as a 'Thumbs up' sign from the universe urging the querent to just damn the consequences and take the plunge. Life is all about taking chances, and we win some, while we lose some. The querent is advised not to be too afraid or lazy to take advantage of the little chances life brings his way.

In the Universal Waite Card, hand is stretching forth from the clouds. The hand emerging from the clouds is interpreted as an unexpected gift that originates from the divine. The divine has just chosen, out of the blue, to bless the querent with a sudden gift. It is now up to the querent to decide if he wants to take advantage of the gift given, or if he wants to ignore it.

In the enclosed hand is a wand that seems to be alive – this passes two important messages; the place of will in the conversion of opportunities to success stories, and the great potential that abounds in some seemingly insignificant gifts. First, no matter how free or unexpected an opportunity is, we still have to be determined to make sure that we find a way to make optimal use of that opportunity.

We may not have been determined to seek out that opportunity, but if the benefits that abound in that opportunity are going to be reaped, then we must be prepared to put in the required efforts. The potentials that abound in a seemingly ordinary opportunity may be enormous. Hence, we must endeavor as much as possible to make maximum use of any chances at success, growth or personal development that we get, because we are never sure how far an 'ordinary' opportunity could get us.

Finally, the cloud in the image signifies the fleeting nature of the opportunity given. The opportunity is represented by an ace, it is only temporary and will not last forever. Therefore, instead of wasting time and contemplating whether to act on it or not, the querent is advised to observe quickly and then take action because time and tide wait for no man.

INTRINSIC CARD MEANING: The Ace of Wands basically informs the querent about a temporary incoming opportunity that will not be available for long, and might serve as an opportunity for career growth, the development of a project, or the advancement of a cause related to the fire element.

TWO OF WANDS

The two of wands simply represents a delicate balance between energy and vision. In our sojourn through life, for true success to be achieved, the right combination of inspiration and effort is extremely critical. Having a vision without taking appropriate efforts to actualize the vision will ensure that an individual's dream perpetually remains a dream. However, summoning the courage, despite all odds being stacked against us, to make efforts towards actualizing our visions helps to put the mechanism of success in motion. It is, however, still extremely important, while working hard to achieve our dreams, to always keep our visions and dreams in focus.

Constantly reminding ourselves of the dreams that spurred us on into taking action in the first place, and how we hope to use our eventual achievements to make the world a better place will help us to stay strong and committed to our dreams in the long run, even when the initial rush to act dies down, and obstacles begin to militate against our success.

In life, therefore, there is a time to identify one's purpose and figure out exactly how we want to make valuable contributions to the cause if changing the world for the better. However, the journey to the discovery of purpose might be a long and tortuous one, and one cannot afford to just spend years waiting for that single magical moment when the picture of one's purpose would just flash into one's mind.

We must constantly keep moving, developing ourselves, and acquiring valuable experience while we continue to ponder on how we can use our lives to benefit humanity. Chances are, while we are actively working on developing ourselves as individuals, it would become clear to us, the actual roles we can play in our immediate environments, to be the change we want to see in the world.

While gathering experience and seeking a vision, it also makes sense to begin to build the mental and physical energy that would be required for the actualization of the vision we are seeking. You may figure out your purpose early, to you may figure it out late. What you cannot afford to begin late, however, is the gathering of energy. As soon as you can, you must begin to amass the energy, drive and determination that you would eventually require to achieve your dreams. Reinforcing your mentality towards success and preparing yourself intellectually for the journey ahead are great ways to gather energy for the actualization of your vision.

There is a time for realizing your vision, and a time for building the energy you would need to pursue your dreams to a logical conclusion. It is important not to confuse the two processes, and not to let one interfere with the other. If the vision has not come to you yet, keep gathering the energy, and actively looking out. When the vision occurs to you through active searching, then the time comes to put all the energy that you have been gathering to good use.

The image on the Universal Waite Card shows the critical importance of balancing vision and energy to the realization of success. There is a man holding the world in one hand – showing the importance of a vision. Visions can be big or small, but the most important characteristic they must possess, is that they must be able to help make the world a better place. The vision must have something to do with the world as a whole. The wand in the man's hand represents the place of will and energy in the actualization of visions.

As has been mentioned many times in this text, success is largely determined by how willing an individual is to try, and keep trying even in the face of daunting challenges. The wand reminds us, as individuals, that after figuring out our visions or purpose in life, we need to work extremely hard and remain dogged to ensure our visions become reality.

In the image, the man is seeing gazing out to the sea ahead of him. This is interpreted as the continuous process of gaining inspiration and energy to keep pushing harder towards the realization of a dream. Inspiration, creativity and energy can be derived from various things and activities, it all depends on how deeply an individual can reason to derive the motivation he requires from even the most mundane, everyday things. Gaining more inspiration on a daily basis is going to ensure the individual keeps his goal in focus at all times, making it easier to work towards the realization of set goals.

The man in the image is seen to steady the wand on a cube decorated with white lilies and red roses. The representation of the wand, symbolizing will on the cube, a steady structure, shows that while we expend our energies and efforts towards the actualization of our goals, we must always keep both our feet grounded in reality. As we work hard to achieve our dreams, we should not get too excited or distracted such that we lose focus and start deviating from our vision. We must work extremely hard, but in a direction that leads straight to the actualization of our goals.

The white lilies adorning the cube signify the purity of the intention if the man with the vision. Having dubious intentions and then working hard towards the realization of selfish or destructive goals is likely to backfire because the intentions of the undertaker of the mission were not pure in the first place. Even if the plans do follow through, the realization if such a dubious goal is not going to help make the world a better place in any way. When we work towards our goals and strive for perfection therefore, we must always review our intentions and make sure that they are still aimed at helping to make an impact on the world, and not just for our own selfish interests.

The red roses symbolize the place of passion in the actualization of dreams. A lot of people have dreams that they are not passionate about. This is common in cases where people are pursuing goals foisted upon them by the society, or when they are just trying to follow the crowd. Before dedicating your time, energy and resources towards the realization of certain goals, it is extremely critical that you be passionate and deeply moved by the goal you are pursuing. This ensures you'll always have the energy to keep pressing forward towards the realization of your goals even when the journey gets impossibly difficult and every fibre of your being tells you to quit.

INTRINSIC MEANING OF THE CARD: This card simply emphasizes the importance of having a vision and building up the energy to actualize that vision.

THREE OF WANDS

The key message of the Three of Wands is active waiting. In life, when we have set all plans towards the actualization of a goal in motion, at some point, we need to exercise some patience for some specific results to materialize. To ensure the success of any endeavor whatsoever, it is important to strike a balance between being proactive and being patient. Active waiting in this context is not just waiting idly for a result to materialize, it involves getting ready for the right moment to take the next action.

The Three of Wands therefore reminds us on the importance of preparedness. While waiting for the golden moment; the exact time to strike, it is essential for you to develop yourself, acquire the necessary resources and put all necessary requirements in place as soon as you can so when the golden moment you are expecting arrives, you will be fully alert and poised, and you will strike when the iron is still hot.

A lot of people make the deadly mistake of procrastinating on getting ready for their opportune moments. Opportunities may only come once, and when lost, they may never be recovered. Whether the moment of opportunity is pre-determined or not, it extremely important to get all things ready as soon as possible so we will be able to strike just when the time is right.

The period of active waiting is described as the one between gathering of energy and realizing a goal. That time window is one that should be characterized by firm belief and increasing readiness. You shouldn't only be preparing yourself to physically strike by getting all resources in place, you should also psychologically strengthen yourself. Remind yourself you are strong, powerful and unstoppable, and that when the moment comes, you will be ready to take maximum advantage of the fleeting opportunity.

In the Universal Waite Card, a figure is standing at a place that looks like a harbor, waiting for the ship that would take him to his desired destination. This signifies that waiting is important. Some things in life just cannot be rushed. Sometimes, even though we want to just move on to the next activity or the next phase of our lives, it is key for us to exercise patience and wait for the right moment before taking action. The numerous wands in the picture signify the place of will and determination in the process of active waiting.

Patience sounds easy, but sometimes, it can actually take more willpower to be patient than not to be. Sometimes, every fibre in your body is telling you to act immediately; to keep moving, but your logical sense tells you that the time to act is not right, and acting right away would only lead to poor results. Therefore, it becomes your responsibility to willfully control your wild innate desires to ensure that you accomplish your goals.

INTRINSIC CARD MEANING: The Three of Wands tells the querent to be patient, but to get themselves poised for action in the process.

FOUR OF WANDS

The Four of Wands represents the final result of a plan; a destination. When we set out with a vision, gather energy and determination, and allow ourselves to be fueled by our inner passion and the purity and nobility of our intentions, we would usually find ourselves arriving at our desired destination against all odds. The Four of Wands tells a querent that the time for the realization of a goal is at hand, and it is time to intensify all efforts to ensure the goal is actually realized.

In the first card, the Ace of Wands, the querent is being told that the opportune, temporary moment to strike, to plant a seed is imminent. In the Four of Wands, the querent is simply being informed that the time to reap the rewards of his efforts is also imminent. The querent is therefore being implored not to quit if any challenges are currently being faced because while the darkest hour may be before dawn, the beauty of sunrise justifies the darkness of the night that precedes it.

In the Universal Waite Card, an atmosphere of general celebration and joy is depicted. The bower of wands and the flower garland on top of it signify the place of will in the realization of the goal being celebrated. If the individual or group had not been determined in their pursuit of their visions, then the intended goals would never have been actualized.

The flower garlands in particular symbolize the fleeting nature of the moment; life is not an eternal celebration. Soon, the celebrations would be over and it would be time for the celebrants and the well-wishes alike to get back to working on other subsequent visions. This reminds us as individuals, of the transient nature of life, and how important it is to relish and treasure the isolated, memorable times.

FIVE OF WANDS

The Five of Wands, as is evident on the image on it, represents conflict and misunderstanding. Conflicts are bound to arise when two or more people are gathered to achieve a single, or multiple goals. No two people are completely wired the same, we all understand other people, statements, actions in different ways, and accordingly respond to varying circumstances in varying ways. Conflict therefore becomes inevitable in everyday life as we try to co-exist with others.

Forms of conflict may range from competition, arising from wanting the same thing, to aggression, when both parties turn on each other with the mutual intent of destruction. The Five of Wands serves to remind us that conflict never has any favorable results, and reminds the querent to always be prepared to find a common ground with an opponent in the case if a conflict. The card advocates the immediate resolution and management of conflicts, because going alone might make us move faster, but working with others as an integral part of a functional team gets us further.

The Five of Cards highlights the destructive effects of protracted conflict in the long and short term and reminds individuals not to hold grudges, but to be solution-oriented in all incendiary situations. The card also reminds us to always look for the silver lining in the cloud of our differences. We may come from different backgrounds and have different ideologies about how certain situations should be handled, but our differences only make us stronger. We must therefore endeavor not to just loom past our differences, but to harness our diversity to foster synergy and build a team that's stronger than the sum of its parts.

In the Universal Waite Card, a group of people are pictured, vying for the same goal. Even though it doesn't seem like an extremely aggressive fight, the element if competition is still there. The wands represent the place of independent wills in every contest; every party is determined to win, despite all odds. The image subtly communicates the importance of finding common ground in all arguments and learning to work together to achieve desired goals, rather than antagonizing each other.

INRINSIC MEANING OF THE CARD: The querent is warned to beware of possible imminent conflict and to be ready to seek solutions instead of aggravating the situation.

SIX OF WANDS

The Six of Wands is a card that celebrates the achievements of one single individual, and not the recognition of a group's efforts. In life, we tend to work extremely hard and tenaciously towards the achievement if our personal goals if we want those dreams to come true bad enough. The reasons why we keep holding on to our dreams may differ – it might be because of the passion we have for the dream; it might be because of our family…we all have different reasons that keep us going in the pursuit of our dreams. The Six od Wands is specially dedicated to the individual, though despite all odds, has stood alone and strong through all the storms that blew against him, till he realized his dreams.

The Six of Wands emphasizes the importance of the limelight in the celebration of the individual involved. He has been laboring on his own for so long, trying to achieve his dreams. Now that he has finally accomplished success, he is not confined to the shadows anymore. His time has finally come to shine. Related to the limelight is the recognition form others. The individual is not just going to celebrate his achievements by himself – he is going to be hugely celebrated and recognized by others for his valiant efforts towards actualizing a dream that would not just help him progress, but would positively influence the life of a lot of people.

In the Universal Waite Card, a man is pictured riding on a horse in a public celebratory setting. The festive atmosphere represents the recognition of the individual's goals by well-wishers. The laurel of wreaths in the image signifies the honor and prestige that the individual has acquired from accomplishing his goals. This serves to remind us as individuals to always keep our goals in focus, and remember the perks that would come with the actualization of our dreams.

The honor bestowed upon the individual would make him even more determined to go on to achieve bigger things. The audience are seen lifting their wands in solidarity. This shows that the audience does not just passively appreciate the celebrant's achievements, they are actually determined to celebrate and honor him for his spirited efforts to make his life and theirs better.

INTRINSIC MEANING OF THE CARD: The querent is to be celebrated for the achievement of a long-deserved goal.

SEVEN OF WANDS

The seven of wands signifies defensiveness. In our everyday life, for several reasons, we may have cause to be on the defensive. We may be trying to defend ourselves against external aggressors, we may be trying to defend our dreams from our own destructive habits, or we may be trying to even defend other people who are being preyed upon by a higher, stronger power. Whatever the motives of our defensiveness are, this card urges us to reconsider our stand, and figure out if being on the defensive is actually worth it.

The Seven of Wands does not specify if the person will win the interpersonal or internal struggle; it just states that the querent will, at some point, have to defend something or someone dear to him. The querent is therefore urged to be strong and unshaken in his efforts to defend what is right, if and only if he has actually figured out that he is in the right position to fight for the cause in question.

Being on the defensive can be a frustrating and debilitating feeling, as a person could constantly feel judged, abused or unfairly treated, and then feel he has had enough and decides to lash out at his aggressors. While being defensive in our daily lives, it is important for our motives not to be to destroy our opponents but to make them understand why we need to be respected, cared for or included in the scheme of things. The aim must be creating a batter status quo, not causing mutually assured destruction.

Defensiveness may not be all bad. It might be an opportunity for an individual to see his own weaknesses and begin the process of growth, development and healing. Being on the defensive is also an avenue for individuals to show uncommon strength and courage while fighting for the cause that they believe in. Defensiveness primes individuals to be strong and determined in the face of a crisis, and face challenges head on, instead of constantly running away from them.

In the Universal Waite Card, the figure is seen to be defending himself from a higher ground using his wand. This signifies the importance of will in the process of defensiveness. If you are not truly determined to protect or defend a person or a cause even in the face of daunting odds, then you are not likely to pursue your defense to a logical conclusion.

Defensiveness requires a sheer amount of willpower and determination to ensure that you conquer your opponents, subdue them, or reach a compromise that at least favors you to an extent. Even though the figure in the picture is defending himself from higher ground; a position of power and authority, defensiveness is not always about crushing rebellions. Sometimes, it's about fighting for one's rights, dreams, or the defense of the helpless and down-trodden.

INTRINSIC MEANING OF THE CARD: The Seven of Wands is a prediction the querent might have to brace himself to defend a person or cause dear to him.

EIGHT OF WANDS

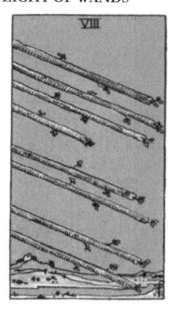

The image on the Eight of Wands shows wands flying through the air. This card, is therefore, all about speed, rapidity, promptness and conciseness of purpose. Know what you want to do, and get it done fast, simple. A lot of people go too slow in life, thinking if they go too fast, they'll burn, but the race of life is not for the weak or the slow. It is our job as individuals with winners' mindsets to act with promptness. You can't go through all your life being slow. While speed without purpose is completely useless, after figuring out exactly what you want, it is important for you to start pursuing your goals as quickly as possible, while putting in the maximum effort possible to ensure you achieve your dreams in time.

In the moments of swiftness, however, we must be careful to keep our feet grounded in reality so we do not lose control of the situation. Our willpower must remain solid while we gun for our dreams as fast as we can.

The Eight of Wands also illustrates the power if sudden outer influences. When pursuing a goal, and we are being too sluggish with it, a rapid outer influence can simply sweep in and take the prize right before our very eyes. On the flipside also, speed can be a very valuable weapon in our arsenal if we are vying for a keenly contested goal. The card is all about the importance if swiftness, and how rapid action can completely change circumstances and expected outcomes.

In the Universal Waite Card, wands are seen moving swiftly through the air, representing events in motion, heading for a conclusion. The wands themselves represent how important it is for you to retain control and determination for the achievement of your goal while of course, reaching

for your dreams as swiftly as you can,
INTRINSIC MEANING OF THE CARD: The querent is urged to proceed rapidly to change the course of events and achieve unprecedented victory. The card also signifies how prompt action can disrupt the status quo.

NINE OF WANDS

The nine of wands simply symbolizes survival. The human spirit is almost infinite in its strength and ability to withstand adversity. While we may all have our personal limits, adversity helps to strengthen us and prepare us for life's constant challenges. The wands being held on to by the figure in the mage symbolize the importance of determination and willpower in the survival of rough times. Giving up might constantly seem like the easy way out, but keeping our goals in focus and remembering we were not born to be average will constantly keep us going, even when we are swimming against the tide.

After undergoing tough times, we are bound to come out stronger, and with an increased capability for endurance and perseverance. Therefore, in a way, tough times are actually required to help us grow and get ready for success. The values of self-reliance, patience, courage and wisdom have been known to come from times of pain and adversity.

It is when you are at your very lowest that you can tap into the deep reserves of your strength and potentials to figure a way out, and you may end up surprising yourself by how much staying power and strength that you actually have. When life doesn't require us to show uncommon courage, we never truly realize how brave we can be.

In the Universal Waite Card, a wounded figure is shown, leaning upon a staff, watching the horizon. The person has faced a strong adversary and survived. He might be physically wounded, but mentally, he has been strengthened, because he now relies on his reinforced determination and willpower to keep moving as he gradually heals. Looking out on the horizon, he is mentally getting prepared for the next challenge coming his way, because he is now confident with how strong he has become.

INTRINCIS MEANING OF THE CARD: The Nine of Wands simply tells the Querent to be strong and steadfast through the strong times, as they are only meant to help him get stronger to tackle upcoming challenges.

TEN OF WANDS

The Ten of Wands is a card that deals with the bearing of necessary burdens. In our personal and professional lives, there are specific responsibilities that would be foisted upon us that we just wouldn't have a choice but to bear. Even though some burdens may not be completely compulsory, still, we may feel obliged to bear them, probably out of respect to a senior colleague, or out of loyalty to a friend. The burdens may also be extremely significant, or may just occur as minor inconveniences. Whatever form a burden takes, the Ten of Wands informs the querent that somewhere along the line, he would actually have to brace up to deal with specific burdens or responsibilities coming his way.

The card doesn't show how the querent should handle the burden, or even is the burden should be bore or simply ignored, but it informs the querent of the existence of the burden in question, and tells him to watch out for it.

In the Universal Waite Card, a figure is pictured carrying a conspicuously inconvenient burden, while heading for a particular destination. This shows us that at times, in life, we may have to stand strong and bear serious responsibilities either for ourselves or for the people we care about. The card tells us burdens and responsibilities are a part of life, and while they might make our journey harder, we must not let them stop us in our tracks as we head for our goals. The burdens are represented as wands. This shows that to efficiently handle all burdens we have to bear; we must be innately willing and prepared to manage our burdens on our own. Achieving something as serious as bearing a burden successfully takes a lot of willpower and dedication.

INTRINSIC MEANING OF THE CARD: The card simply warns the querent of the possibility of having to deal with necessary burdens.

ACE OF CUPS

The Ace of Cups is the first card of the 'Cups' suit. As has been stated earlier, the cards of the cups suit usually pass messages related to the element 'water' – dealing with day-to-day management of relationships, intuition, creativity and spirituality.

The ace, in all suits, always represents a gift or an unexpected opportunity that never lasts forever. The ace of cups represents a fortuitous point in time fraught with infinite possibility, but must be harnessed swiftly lest it passes just as quickly as it came. The point of the Ace if Cups is for querents to be on the lookout for opportunities for new chances at spiritual awakening, strengthening their responsibilities, or sharpening their intuition and creativity. Inspirations that breed creativity are usually very rapid – they arrive in the blink of an eye, and within moments, they might be lost. The querent is therefore advised to seize the day and take quick advantage of opportunities that life brings his way.

The Ace of Cups urges us as individuals to sometimes choose our hearts over complex logic. Sometimes, it might not fully make sense, especially in cases of love and intuition, but we might just have to trust our guts and give new chances a try. Maybe we might end up getting our hearts broken, or maybe we might create timeless masterpieces or find timeless love. Either way, the message of the Ace of Wands is 'Take a leap of faith.'

In the Universal Waite Card, there is chalice with a catholic –like look. It shows that concepts such as love, inspiration and spiritual awakening are tied to the divine, and these chances are only bestowed to selected beings once in a blue moon. There are therefore chances that should be made maximum use of. The hand emerging from the clouds shows that the opportunity is a gift, while the clouds show the fleeting nature of the gift being offered. If it is not fully maximized soon, it will be taken away.

INTRINSIC MEANING OF THE CARD: The querent is simply being advised to look out for opportunities for emotional experiences and growth, and to utilize those opportunities as fast as possible before they quickly become unavailable.

TWO OF CUPS

The Two of Cups signifies the imminence of a new relationship, a new form of emotional excitement or a deep attraction. The Two of Cups also serves a symbol of the coming of a deep connection, or the deepening of an existing connection between friends, colleagues or even teachers and students. In our journey through life as individuals, at specific points, we stumble into circumstances of events that put our relationships and connections with people dear to us to test. When we emerge and the relationship survives this test, the relationship usually emerges stronger and probably ends up to be a life-long one. In other circumstances, tough times may bring us in contact with people we end up having incredible long-term relationships with.

In other cases, the circumstances that help to deepen or establish a life-long relationship may not be necessarily traumatic or devastating; they may actually be pleasant. The point of the Two of Cups, however, is that a situation is about to arise that will lead to the establishment of a deep relationship between the querent and another person. The Two of Cups, however, doesn't specify exactly how long the impending relationship or connection will last.

In the Universal Waite Card, how the strengths of relationships are based on powerful emotional bonds are illustrated. The two figures in the card as seeing to pose with dignity and poise, and their union signifies healing. When some powerful relationships are established, the bond shared by the two parties tends to help heal long-term wounds bore by one or both parties. The Two of Cups signifies the impending relationship will help to bring healing and peace. The Caduceus in the image; the wand, signifies the power of will in keeping the emotional connections alive.

If a relationship is going to survive, both parties must be prepared to keep the fires of the emotional connection they share burning. The Lion with wings represents the basal animalistic tendencies humans tend to exhibit when they are in love, or under the influence if a powerful emotional connection. It has been said that love has the power to bring out the angel or demon in a person.

INTRINSIC MEANING OF THE CARD: The Two of Cups signifies the establishment of a new relationship.

THREE OF CUPS

The Three of Cups card simply signifies joy and happiness that is sudden and usually unexpected. Joy and happiness are feelings that everybody wants in their lives, but when these feelings come with a wave of spontaneity, it even makes the feeling more treasurable, and the moments more memorable. The Three of Cups does not signify what will bring the joy to the querent, but it signifies that moments of unplanned bliss are on the way. The card does not also specify how enormous the happiness and joy would be.

Family gatherings are significant moments of deep joy and bonding. Relatives who have spent a long time apart come together and bond over memories, past experiences, and situations they have faced while apart from each other. The bond of family keeps them together even when they are apart, and when they finally get the chance to get together, the joy is usually almost palpable in the air. The kind of pure, unadulterated joy gotten from family gatherings is represented by the Three of Cups. You never plan to experience so much bliss just catching up with family, but when you eventually find yourself with them, the joy just erupts.

The Three of Cups also signifies goodwill and contentment in the moments of bliss. Sometimes, when we experience unprecedented blessings, we are not completely satisfied with the extent of the joy that has come our way. That is not the case in the situation predicted by the Three of Cups. The Three of Cups predicts joy that brings contentment and satisfaction. The Three of Cups also suggests that the incoming bliss is going to be a shared experience, not a lone one. The joy is going encompass a group of people, and their individual feelings if happiness are going to make the group's success even more stupendous.

In the Universal Waite Card, the pumpkins and grapes in the image signify abundance, and the inexplicable joy and inspiration that can come from even the simplest successes. The grapes and pumpkins simply symbolize that the bliss would be immense, and the querent's joy will be pure and unadulterated. The three women lifting the cups signify that the joy is going to spread over a group of people, and the mutually shared affection is going to make the experience of bliss even more incredible. The festive atmosphere depicted in the image signifies the celebration that would accompany the happiness that is about to be experienced. The querent is going to be celebrated with for the unexpected wave of joy that he is about to experience.

INTRINSIC MEANING OF THE CARD: Sudden, unprecedented bliss.

FOUR OF CUPS

The Four of Cups card represents the feeling of discontentment with prevailing circumstances. Several time in our emotional lives and in our relationships, we feel unsatisfied with the status quo. Our dissatisfaction with the current state of a relationship may stem from the fact that things used to be better, or we feel that things should actually be better. We may feel our partner is not putting in enough efforts to make the relationship work smoothly. We may even feel angry that our significant other is exhibiting habits that are weakening the integrity of the relationship. For whatever reason it is that we feel unsatisfied with a relationship or prevailing circumstances, the Four of Cups reminds us to always put in our best to make valuable relationships work and learn to overlook the mistakes of the ones we care for.

Being dissatisfied with a relationship or current circumstances in one's personal life may have positive or negative effects. On the positive side, dissatisfaction may motivate a person to work harder on a relationship to make it work, despite all odds. On the negative side, however, discontentment with a relationship or a circumstance may cause a person to become depressed and abandon the cause altogether, or even act out and ruin the little progress he had made so far.

Therefore, the Four of Cups reminds us to be mindful of our actions when we are not happy with prevailing circumstances or results achieved. The Four if Cups does not specify what action a querent should take to deal with an unsatisfactory relationship – it just states the querent is likely to feel discontented with a circumstance in the foreseeable future.

In the Universal Waite Card, an image of a man with a set of cups placed before him, looking unhappy is depicted. This signifies that the querent may have to choose from a variety if unpleasant options. In the image, a hand is presenting a cup to the figure; representing a fresh new option that may be a solution. But the figure seems to have lost interest in even choosing, which is what happens when a person refuses to look for ways to solve a problem but chooses to sulk about it instead. Or the figure may not notice the cup, which is another thing that might happen when someone is not putting in the necessary efforts to salvage a failing relationship, or a deteriorating situation. In all, the Four of Cups tells the querent about an impending unpleasant situation, and advise him to manage it wisely.

INTRINSIC MEANINF OG THE CARD: The Four of Cups signifies discontentment with available options or prevailing circumstances.

FIVE OF CUPS

The Five of Cups signifies an experience of profound loss and grief. In life, at one point or the other, we are bound to experience the pain associated with losing something or someone dear to us. As we go through life, we lose friends, family, property, opportunities, money and other things special to us. In these moments, we are prone to despondence, depression, and are highly vulnerable.

The Five of Cups card does not specify what might cause, grief, or what would be left after loss has been experienced. The Five of Cups instead focuses on the feeling of grief, and how hard it can be to come to terms with losing someone or something extremely special. The card lets the querent understand that losing something dear can leave a terribly huge void that can a very long time to fill, or may never even be filled, ever.

In the period of mourning, people react differently. Some people express their grief physically, letting out the pain by crying, reliving memories they created with the lost person or thing. Some people keep the pain in and try to be strong while trying to comfort other affected people. They may not have a choice than to react this way, because the onus has now fallen on them to help others find strength in the midst of the calamity, and they themselves cannot afford to breakdown. Some people do not allow themselves to process the grief, they just shut out all the feelings and struggle to move on. The problem is, they never really move on. The grief continues to weigh on heavily in their subconscious because they never allow it to get processed and pass.

The Five of Cups reminds us as individuals that grief and loss in life is inevitable. Just as we'd have moments of bliss and inexplicable joy, so will times of devastation and loss come. The Five of Cups reminds us that it's normal to mourn and grieve, instead of numbing our minds to the pain. The card also reminds us to pick ourselves back up and keep moving.

In the Universal Waite deck, the Five of Cups displays an image depicting the phases of grief. The figure's back is turned, indicating denial. Most individuals, when first informed about a loss, or experiencing it first-hand, go straight into denial. They'll tell themselves: "It cannot be. It did not happen. This is just a nightmare. I will undo this mess." But as they try in vain to deny the truth of the loss they suffer; they move on to the next phase; anger.

This phase is depicted by the cups that have been kicked all over the place by the querent in his fit of anger and frustration. A lot of people act out when experiencing loss. They may smash items close to them in the wall, throw things out of the window, punch the wall with their fists, attempt to beat someone up, or even attempt suicide. It is okay to be angry; the pain has to flow out somehow. It doesn't make sense keeping all the negative energy bottled up inside you. However, if you must shut, scream and cry, do so, but try as much as possible not to harm yourself or become destructive in the period of grief. In the end, people end up regretting actions taken when angry.

The Universal Waite card also depicts the final stage of grief – coming to terms with the situation, getting depressed, and looking to find the bright side in all the mess. This is the stage when people fully accept the loss, contemplate available choice, and begin their process of healing. This process is perhaps the hardest and most critical aspect of grief. If this phase is not fully completed, an individual may find himself scarred for life. Allow yourself to feel the pain; let it course through you. Will yourself to calm down, and begin the process of figuring a path forward. You will eventually look back at your experiences and thank yourself for choosing to heal.

INTRINSIC MEANING OF THE CARD: The card predicts an experience of pain and sorrow, especially in a relationship or emotional circumstance.

SIX OF CUPS

The Six of Cups is drastically different from its predecessor; it symbolizes blissful memories. A lot of people firmly believe that the past holds no sway over the future, but the past can have very powerful effects on how cautious we are around certain people and in certain circumstances, decisions we make, people we relate with and trust, and how we make important choices. Happy memories are some of life's most important treasures, they remind us of great times, and can help us find the strength to move on when the going gets tough. They also remind us to keep working towards perpetual happiness and joy.

The Six of Cups could also symbolize that the querent is about to create happy memories alone, or with other people. Interpreting the Six of Cups in the context of the question asked by the querent makes it extremely easier to decipher its true meaning.

In the Universal Waite Card, a scene of happiness and true cheerfulness is depicted. The white flowers in the cups depict innocent delights; happiness that is not tainted with guilt or shadiness, or a gift that is given without any attached conditions. Most times, in life to be happy and get what we truly want, we have to make sacrifices and compromises. The Six of Cups signifies a type of glee that comes from experiencing true happiness without paying the hefty price of compromising other important things. The tranquil and relaxing atmosphere depicted in the image signifies the feeling of recalling a past that was filled with fun and true joy, a type of feeling that we hope to experience again.

Intrinsic meaning of the card: The Six of Cups signifies the recalling of happy memories.

SEVEN OF CUPS

The Seven of Cups is simply a representation of our innermost wants and desires as individuals. As we grow in life, we tend to want different things at different times. People vary in their approaches to actualizing their dreams – some people give it their all; they get extremely committed to actualizing their dreams and they never let anything stand in their way. Other people take a more lackadaisical path – they choose to be slow and take whatever life throws at them.

The Seven of Cups, however, serves to remind us as dreamers with desires, that our imaginations can be our most powerful tool, and our most critical undoing. While dreaming about your goals, you must learn to keep the path to your dreams in focus. Plan all the way to the end. Know the options you will have to choose from beforehand, weigh them all objectively, and pick a line of action that will lead you straight to the life of your dreams.

The Seven of Cups also indicates that sometimes, we might even have to choose between several dreams- several goals and plans. Some people have the potential to achieve a lot, but they can't do it all at the same time, so they need to pick their priorities and work towards them one at a time. Picking the next goal to pursue might also be a tricky decision to make.

The Seven of Cups does not serve to tell a querent how to choose a dream to pursue, or how to achieve his goals, it only states the feelings associated with being faced with a myriad of options. When there are several routes for you to take towards achieving the life of your dreams, you will not be able to fully focus on the journey until you pick a path to follow. The Seven of Cups therefore reminds us as individuals to pick it paths as soon as we can. We must not rush into making decisions that would influence the rest of your lives, but we must also not tarry too much, lest the moment of opportunity passes us by.

In the Universal Waite Card, a darkened figure is shown with its back turned indicating puzzlement and the need to make a choice. When choosing a dream to pursue, or a path towards achieving a specific a dream, it is common for individuals to be distracted and confused, especially when trying to compare available options. The man is stuck in a shadow looming large above him. This depiction shows how our dreams can tend to overwhelm us when we are still thinking of how to achieve them. As time goes on, however, and we work on actualizing our dreams, we get more accustomed to the feeling of success and achievement. Finally, the contrast between the man and the cups shows the significant difference between the present and the future in focus. When we desire things, it is because we want out future to be better than the present. The Seven of Cups reminds the querent if she sticks to his dreams and fights for them, he would have a future much brighter and pleasant than his present.

INTRINSIC MEANING OF THE CARD: The Seven of Cups simply indicates the importance of dreams and goals.

EIGHT OF CUPS

In the image depicted on the Eight of Cups card of the Universal Waite deck, a man is leaving an ordered row of cups. In the row of cups being abandoned, an open space can be observed in the top row, indicating a missing piece. As we journey through our individual lives, we arrive at points in time where we just need something in particular. At that point, it doesn't matter what we currently have, or what we could have if we keep towing our current path.

What we require at that point is very specific, and we are going to be particular about it. When a couple get married for instance, and decide that it is time for them to have kids, and they cannot, all they want at that time is a kid. It doesn't matter if they have a spectacular mansion or a fleet of exotic cars – all they want at that point is a child.

The Eight of Cups reminds us, when seeking something, to keep in mind all our blessings, but not to forget to pursue our desires relentlessly. The Eight of Cups also signifies leaving one's comfort zone. The figure in the card owns so much cups, but for that single one he desires, he is prepared to leave all he has accumulated to go find his missing piece. Never get too comfortable, never get too relaxed. Keep finding new ways to challenge and improve yourself. That's the message of the Eight of Cups.

The first step on the journey to change is leaving your current position. It doesn't matter if you believe you are all set for life, or of you are at the lowest point of your life. You need to take a step, and then get committed to keeping your journey continued. What drives us to keep pursuing our dreams in life with pronounced tenacity is the promise of transformation;

the hope of change to a better life. We must therefore keep our desires alive in our minds, and feed our focus and drive with thoughts of how the end is eventually going to justify all our struggles.

In the Universal Waite Card, the mountains in the background signify the tpu8gh journey ahead. If your dreams are worthwhile, them the journey towards actualizing them is not going to be a walk in the park. But because you owe it to yourself, your dreams and to every single person who has ever believed in you and supported you, you do not have a choice but to keep forging ahead, no matter the enormity of the obstacles you have to surmount. Always remember that before life hands you anything worthwhile, you have to earn it first; you have to pay the price.

The Moon in the image is final factor to be considered. In Tarot, the moon is almost synonymous with change and unpredictability. Whether you try hard or not, life is going to go on. If you work tirelessly towards achieving your dreams, you may or may not achieve them. What is certain however, is if you do not pursue your desires, you will never have them. So, a change is going to happen; it is imminent. Whether it will be a positive or negative one, is going to largely depend on the efforts you expend in the present.

INTRINSIC MEANING OF THE CARD: The card tells the querent he would have to leave his current position to pursue bigger dreams.

NINE OF CUPS

The Nine of Cups signifies the state of well-being in all ramifications of life – material, physical and emotional perfection. Leading a completely perfect life at all times may not be very feasible. The way life works is that we almost always have to battle with one challenge or the other at various times in our lives. However, this card tells us that true happiness, joy and delight comes from being contented with what you currently have. Of course the Nine of Cups is not asking the querent to become complacent and give up on his goals, the card is only reminding us all that to be truly happy, we must learn to imbibe the values of satisfaction and finding peace in the little we have. Greed, covetousness and inordinate ambition only build walls of bitterness and hate in an individual's mind that eventually prevent him from achieving the success he so badly desires.

In the Universal Waite Card, a conspicuously satisfied figure is seen seated before an admirable collection of beautiful chalices. The chalices in this image indicate the man's achievements till date, and he is taking some time out, to appreciate his successes. Contentment comes from appreciation. If you do not see any value in everything that you have managed to accrue till date, even if you have gotten the whole world, it would still never seem enough. This card reminds us to take some time out every now and then to take stock of our lives – look out how much we have achieved and actually give thanks for how far we have come.

The cups are not just stacked haphazardly or placed on just any surface; they are placed on a table draped in blue velvet. This shows that the man not only appreciates his blessings, he treasures them and cherishes them.

This boosts satisfaction and happiness. Take care of what you have, and watch it, and you blossom. A lot of people accumulate so much, but they do not treasure or maintain what they have, so they just keep struggling for more, hopeful that one day, they would magically find one thing that would eventually bring them true happiness, However, that will not happen, at least not until they learn to truly treasure the blessings that have been bestowed on them.

Finally, in the image, the man is seen to be facing outwards, and not focusing on his possessions. He admires his achievements and cherishes them, but he is not so obsessed with them as to forget other important things in life. This reminds us not to get too pompous or self-absorbed when we begin to experience success in different spheres of our lives, The Nine of Cups reminds us to stay humble, receptive to new people and ideas, and to never give up on our dreams.

INTRINSIC MEANING OF THE CARD: The Nine of Cards simply reflects happiness and well-being stemming from contentment and appreciation.

TEN OF CUPS

The Ten of Cups signifies a happy home. A truly happy home is not made up of just a fancy building or expensive furniture and appliances – a true home is a fortress from which members of a family that love and support each other emerge every day to go ahead to conquer their daily challenges. Like every soldier needs a base of operations; a place to retire to when the battle gets too heated, and a place to celebrate little victories, so does every person who hopes to achieve success in the world, need a place to come home; a place to retire to after a hard day's work, a place to create happy memories, and a place to celebrate life's significant moments.

The home also serves as safe place – a place where protection and rejuvenation is assured. Sometimes, life beats us down, life drives us to our knees. Having a place to call home gives us an opportunity to recover in the presence of the most special people to us in the world, and after we heal, the home gives us the boost of courage we need to go back out and tackle life once again.

A good home is all about stability and unbreakable bonds. Therefore, no matter what an individual achieves in the outside world, he must always strive to keep his home in order, and the foundations that keep the home standing as strong as possible. A lot of people grow up to become distant from their family, and even when they achieve immense success, they still feel empty inside. The home brings an inimitable type of warmth and joy to the heart; therefore, the home must be preserved to keep that warmth alive.

No matter how much we cherish the home however, it still represents our comfort zone, and that means we must take care of it, but we must constantly leave it to explore challenges and achieve our goals. The home is a place to recover, heal, rejuvenate and celebrate, not a place to perpetually remain in. Some people may interpret the home as a symbol of boredom and complacency especially if they cherish danger and intense circumstances. The main point to note, however, is the integrity of the home must be preserved, but the home should not be a permanent hiding place. You still need to go out and fight your battles.

In the Universal Waite Card, adults in the image are seeing raising their hands up, looking skywards. Experts interpret this to represent the role of the divine in the creation of a happy home. And really, what's a home without a belief that keeps the family going in times of crisis? Without a solid belief system to hold the home together, it is likely to break apart very swiftly. Therefore, a common belief in the divine helps to keep a home going even during the tough, dark times.

In then image on the card, kids are seen dancing and playing excitedly. This depicts the true, incomparably bliss that comes from having a stable, functional home. Some families are torn apart due to various factors: selfishness, avarice, lack of compassion, pride, and so on, and the people who from this family may accomplish a lot, but they will never be truly happy because they are disconnected from the basic unit of the society – a stable, loving home.

The rive in the image shows how the relationship shared by members of a family helps nourish their lives. When a family shares a strong bond, the relationships between them will keep them strong even in the face of trouble and help them to tackle life's challenges with boldness because they know they are never alone.

ACE OF SWORDS

The ace of swords like all other aces in the Tarot deck, represents a moment of opportunity; a point in time laden with incomparable potential. However, the ace also represents the temporariness of the situation; if the opportunity is not properly utilized in time, the moment is soon gone for good. The Ace of Swords also features the swift, air-like energy of the swords, symbolizing the importance of logic, intelligence, communication, solving problems and making key, important decisions.

In the Ace of Swords card of the Universal Waite deck, the sword is seen to be pointing skywards. This symbolizes a connection with the divine. When opportunities come, most people believe that it is because God, or the supernatural realm had a degree of control over the emergence of that opportunity. Therefore, the querent may be advised to pray about the opportunity while he gets ready to strike the moment the right time arrives.

The laurel wreath and the olive branch placed on the crown symbolize victory and peace that comes from making the right decisions in the right moments, and solving problems when they come up to prevent further complications. The crown itself portrays authority, dignity and mastery of the art of making critical decisions to take advantage of important opportunities. The crown provides the legitimacy to command the actions of the sword.

The Crown simply reminds us that to take important decisions or solve particular problems, at times, we may need to be in a particular position of power or authority. So if we find ourselves in a position of power, and realize that we have the capability to make a lasting positive difference, we should endeavor to put our authority to good use.

INTRINSIC MEANING OF THE CARD: The Ace of Swords simply tells the querent that an opportunity in the realm of ideas and problem-solving is at hand. The querent must therefore be prepared to act as soon as the moment arrives.

TWO OF SWORDS

The Two of Swords represents a conflict of interest between an individual's heart and his mind. In several decisions we have to make in life, we usually have to decide whether to go with our logic, or follow the whims of our heart. The truth remains that while logic may be a very reliable tool to make critical decisions, some of the most important decisions to be made in life defy logic, and in those circumstances, you just need to follow your heart. So, it is very important for you as a progressive individual to manage to strike a balance between being logical and emotional.

However, in situations where your logical and your emotional side are in a very fierce tussle, you may be left paralyzed and utterly puzzled trying to find common ground between the two opposite alternatives your emotional and logical senses are offering you. This state of confusion can further worsen the situation at hand, because you'll be forced to delay the decision, and this may lead to damage than you could have ever anticipated. While it is not advisable to rush into making important decisions, swift choices are still required in many cases, and as an individual, you need to learn how think decisively under pressure and arrive at a decision that will ensure your well-being in the long run.

The card does not state how long the struggle between the querent's logical and emotional side would last, or which side he should go with. However, since the Swords suit is all about logic and making well-thought out decisions, it is widely believed this card is an indication that the querent needs to think very deeply about an impending decision, and not make major choices based on fleeting emotions.

In the Universal Waite Card, a woman is pictured sitting on a bench, holding two swords. This indicates a situation when we have to choose between two opposing alternatives. Achieving a compromise is hard, and choosing one option would represent choosing logic over emotions, while choosing the second who represent putting one's emotions first. The Blindfold on the woman's face, however, ensures that she cannot see the two swords in her hands, hence she cannot be swayed the sword's appearance, which may persuade her to get emotional.

The absence of sight in the making of the decisions means the woman has to use logic to choose the stronger, more powerful sword. Behind the blindfolded woman is the sea and the moon, both of which indicate the importance of the heart and our emotions in even the most logical decisions we make. Even though the woman has been blindfolded to eradicate all kinds of bias as she makes the important decision, somehow, her heart still plays a role in the decision-making process.

INTRINSIC MEANING OF THE CARD: The Two of Swords simply represents the constant struggle we face in life to choose between our heart and our mind's impulses.

THREE OF SWORDS

The Three of Swords is a card that represents distress or regret caused by the knowledge of something. The proverb 'Ignorance is bliss' is one that has been around for centuries, and is still used very frequently because of how relatable it is to all individuals regardless of age or social status. What you do not know cannot hurt you. However, the moment you are informed of a devastating piece of information, you get despondent and sorrowful, Sometimes, however, the bliss of ignorance may even be more dangerous, because by the time you realize the truth, the situation may have deteriorated beyond the possibility of repair.

In the Universal Waite Card, three swords are depicted in the image, showing the three stages of pain caused by realizing a hurtful fact, or learning about a devastating piece of information. First of all, the individual experience an immediate surge of pain – debilitating and almost overwhelming in its severity. However, as the truth sinks in, the individual realizes he has to face reality. So acceptance of the fact that the pain has occurred is represented by the second sword. The third sword represents a careful appraisal of the situation, and the realization that what has happened is unchangeable, and that an aspect of the individual's life would now be different forever. This applies to situations where an event or action leads to a permanent consequence.

In the card, the three swords stab a heart, representing the immense pain that sometimes accompanies the truth – such as the news of death or the realization of a betrayal. It hurts terribly and weakens the concerned individual. The heavens are also seen to be shedding tears in the card –

indicating the helplessness of the whole situation, and how nothing can be done to remedy the damage that has already been caused. Moving on would be terribly difficult, but since nothing can be done to reverse the effects, the individual just needs to find a way to keep going.

INTRINSIC MEANING OF THE CARD: The pain of the hurt that knowledge can cause.

FOUR OF SWORDS

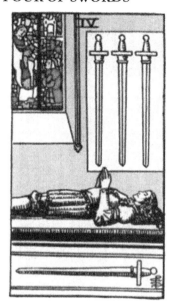

The Four of Swords represents relief, however temporary from struggles and tribulations. Trouble comes in different forms at different points in an individual's life. Some problems are extremely critical and urgent, requiring immediate solutions. Some are more chronic and complicated, requiring in-depth thought, reflection, and even external consultations in some cases. Whatever type of problem an individual is dealing with, handling trouble is exhausting and tasking regardless.

When faced with a very pressing problem, it consumes all your time and attention, takes away your happiness and peace of mind, and leaves you constantly distraught. Tough problems have the capability to physically, mentally, and emotionally exhaust us as individuals, and it is always a refreshing experience to be relieved of our problems, even if the respite gained is only temporary.

Getting a time-out while battling a problem may enable you as an individual to relax, get your act together and critically examine the problem from a new perspective without the pressure of having to deal with the problem head-on. Temporary breaks from a struggle can help an individual to figure out a new plan of action that can eventually help lead to a permanent resolution. Tranquility and peace help to calm the mind and encourage it to explore new ways to solve a problem.

In the Universal Waite Card, a man can be seeing lying in a church. The church represents a temporary haven from whatever he is running from, or struggling with. The church also symbolizes the impact of the divine and higher wisdom. When we have the opportunity as individuals to gain reprieve from our struggles, we are suddenly empowered with the ability to think better and be more focused on solving the problem. Keeping God in the loop may also help solve your problem faster because you would constantly have the belief that you are not alone, and that is enough to bolster your confidence to keep trying harder.

The casket in the image symbolizes death, however, death in this situation refers to the eventual end of an age-long tribulation. Getting a temporary reprieve from a tortuous struggle can help an individual find the necessary insight needed to end the problem once and for all.

INTRINSIC CARD MEANING: The Four of Swords simply represents temporary reprieve from one's tribulations, allowing deep thought and a permanent solution.

FIVE OF SWORDS

The Five of Swords card represents pyrrhic victories. Some victories are won on a platter of gold; they cost us almost nothing. Of course any significant achievement must come with sacrifice — sacrifices of time, energy, effort and resources mostly. However, a pyrrhic victory comes at an extremely unpleasant cost that might even be more devastating than the pain of the original problem that was solved. The only great thing about pyrrhic victories is that a long-raging storm has finally been ended, and an individual, or a group of people can finally embark on the journey to healing. The cost of the solution is, however, usually terribly enormous. Sometimes, pyrrhic victories come with such great costs that they are sometimes referred to as epic losses, especially when the price paid for the victory is higher than the benefits reaped.

In life sometimes, we need to accept pyrrhic victories and just keep moving while hoping for better days ahead. Pyrrhic victories may be achieved in our personal, professional or emotional lives. We must come to terms with the fact that what has been lost is gone, and we must learn to take refuge in the fact we won, even if we had to pay a great price for it. We must them take steps to ensure terrible situations like the ones that have debilitated us do not happen again.

The image on the Five of Swords Card in the Universal Waite Deck is a depiction of a figure who is visibly happy despite having suffered a loss. The figure has chosen to take refuge in the fact that while he might have lost something dear, he still achieved something great. The message here is simple. Focus on the positives, and never let any situation stop you from

moving forward.
INTRINSIC MEANING OF THE CARD: The Five of Swords simply communicates the message of victory tainted with a heavy loss. The querent is being infirmed to be wary of a possible victory or win that would come at a great price.

SIX OF SWORDS

In life, sometimes, we need other people. While it is true that you are the only person you can fully count on, there will come times in life when you wouldn't be able to handle tricky r devastating situations by yourself. These are the times when you need true friends. The Six of Swords card communicates the message of finding strength in the arms of true friends during a tribulation, and getting out of that problem with the aid of the ones who choose to stand by your side through the dark times.

Trouble has a way of filtering the chaff from the wheat when it comes to true and fake friends. It is easy to call someone your friend, or claim to be someone's friend. However, when the going gets tough, then you realize who exactly truly has your best interests at heart. The Six of Swords also communicates the message of giving up; leaving a troubled situation with the help of a trusted one. Of course, we are constantly told never to give up. While perseverance may be a key ingredient to success, sometimes you need to leave to ensure that you live to fight another day. It is therefore very important for you to consider all your options and choose the one that ensures self-preservation in the long term.

In the Universal Waite Card, a message of hopelessness and despair is passed. The atmosphere is generally dull, dreary and bleak. The sky is icy and pale with drab clouds, and the figure in the image is cloaked, hiding his true feelings of pain and hurt, and his back is hunched, showing that he is spent, tired and in desperate need of help. The boat and the oarsman in it signify much needed help that has come to the figure in distress.

Of course the figure doesn't want to take the help that has come freely to him. He wants to go on fighting and struggling, but it is general knowledge if he goes on fighting, he would only end up worse. Even he himself probably knows deep inside that getting out is the best logical option, but the thoughts of what he has lost, and what he might stand to gain, if he wins by a shred of luck, tend to keep him going. The Swords in the image signify war or trouble – the hunched passenger figure has been in a very fierce battle with quite formidable forces, and now that all is almost lost, he has to leave, even though he doesn't want to. The boat leaving the trouble and chaos in the background behind signifies the human ability to move on, away from our troubles and struggles towards calmer waters and a brighter, more stable future.

Of course, it's never easy leaving a fight behind especially when you have so much to gain and have lost so much, but sometimes, you need to consider your own best interests, the risks involved, and the people dear to you and just walk away. This card signifies giving up a chance at glory for the sake of self-preservation.

INTRINSIC MEANING OF THE CARD: The card simply signifies leaving a chaotic or dangerous circumstance with the help of a trusted ally.

SEVEN OF SWORDS

This card symbolizes the distasteful act of theft. All over the world, and in all civilizations in history, thieves are despised and hated. They tale what is not theirs and leave the owners in pain and despair. The Seven of Swords does not indicate what is to be stolen and who will steal, but it just predicts a form of theft in the querent's life. The card also shows the possibility of the thief's capture. However, the card is not about ideal justice leading to the thief's punishment, the card is more about Karma and reaping the consequences of one's action.

The Universe is just a random, haphazard system as a lot of people think, and while the thief might get away with some heists, eventually he would be caught, and severely punished. The card symbolizes the place of retribution in the flow of the universe. Injustice may go on for a long time, but the truth eventually catches up with every criminal, and the punishment for the thief's crimes would be enormous.

The Swords in the card indicate that the stolen entity doesn't necessarily have to be a material item – it is instead more likely to be an idea, or an intangible asset like an individual's freedom to act. You may wonder, how can someone steal another person's confidence? It's pretty easy. Imagine being slightly skeptical about the possibility of the success of a business idea. A more experienced colleague in the field gets a hold of your idea and using his own assets, does his investigations, and realizes that your idea is golden.

Instead of encouraging you, the colleague comes to you and tells you the business is not feasible, completely shattering your hopes and your confidence to act. You respect his words because of his wealth of experience and move on while he makes a fortune from your ideas by robbing you of your confidence. Freedom, communicative abilities and the authority to make decisions are other important intangible entities that may be stolen.

In the Universal Waite Card, the thief is shown to be brightly dressed, and prancing in the daylight without any iota of stealth or secrecy. This image shows the careless of a lot of thieves. They are not usually smart enough to come up with their own ingenuous ideas, but they are neither smart enough to even steal properly either. The thief is portrayed as careless and reckless, and he is soon caught and severely punished.

The two swords left behind by the thief show that the evidence that he leaves in his trail is going to eventually be the weapon that will be used to nail him. The thief is not careful nor covert. The most important job for the thief is to cover his tracks properly, but this thief is way too lazy to do anything properly, and he is soon apprehended.

INTRINSIC MEANING OF THE CARD: The card simply symbolizes the detestable act of taking someone else's property (material or intellectual) unduly.

EIGHT OF SWORDS

This card symbolizes a dangerous or precarious situation. As individuals, we vary in our abilities to remain calm and collected under pressure. However, as the Eight of Swords symbolizes, the ability to remain stable and undaunted even in the face of immense danger is a critical factor to success in everyday life. From time to time, we are faced with very challenging situations, and in those moments, the enormity of the prevailing circumstances tends to makes us fidgety and nervous. However, being unstable is the worst thing that can happen to a person under pressure, because being anxious makes you extremely susceptible to making a grievous, irrevocable mistake.

The message of the Eight of Swords is simple, when you are in danger or faced with a seemingly insurmountable challenge, your first task is to stay calm. Don't fret, and do not panic. Keep a cool head, seek for help if you need it, but you must not go into panic mode. As long as you keep a cool head and do not succumb to the pressure, chances are you will make it through the dangerous situation you are in. If you are panic, however, you will probably blow it and regret your lack of control over yourself for a very long time.

The Eight of Swords also communicates the message of feeling inhibited and restrained. When we feel caged, our normal human instinct is to lash out; to fight back against the forces holding us captive or limiting us. We cannot move as freely and swiftly as we desire, and we hate it. The message is the same as to the person in danger – keep your calm and tackle the situation with a calm disposition. Keeping your emotions under control and choosing logic will get you through.

In the Universal Waite Card, the woman in the image is depicted to be caged; surrounded by a plethora of swords. She cannot move forwards or backwards – she is danger, and has been effectively mobilized. However, despite her incredibly precarious situation, she stays calm and in control, simply waiting for the right time to strike. Therefore, as individuals feeling trapped or in danger, the key to freedom and eventual success is not being nervous, afraid or angry – it is remaining calm while everyone around you is losing their heads, and finding a logical solution in the face of great danger.

INTRINSIC MEANING OF THE CARD: The card simply symbolizes the importance of being calm in dangerous situations.

NINE OF SWORDS

The Nine of Swords communicates a very powerful message – a message that has been in circulation within the human race for centuries, and is still being communicated today because a lot of people are not adhering to this message. The message is 'do not worry'. In life, we all cry too much over spilt milk. We regret missed opportunities, lost chances at glory, lost shots at success. Instead of figuring out a way to move on and keep pushing on, we allow ourselves to get caught up in the reverie of what could have been. However, we must train ourselves to be better than that. What has happened has happened, and as a progressive individual, it is now your responsibility to move on. So, leave it all behind, do not obsess over what has been lost and just keep moving.

Thinking constantly about what has been lost or what could have been is a very dangerous delay factor. Not letting go prevents you from moving forward – your mind is held captive to the negative thoughts running through it, and no matter how hard you try to progress, if you do not let go of worry and regret first, you would only find yourself running around in circles.

In the Universal Waite Card, a figure is pictured in bed, but instead of resting, and giving herself a chance at healing and rejuvenation so that she can have a shot at moving forward, she is feeding her insecurities. She is thinking about what has been lost and cannot be recovered, and is effectively robbing herself of peace and tranquility. The message is simple – what has happened has happened, let it go and give yourself a chance to heal and progress.

INTRINSIC MEANING OF THE CARD: The querent is being warned of the dangers of stagnation that comes with regret.

TEN OF SWORDS

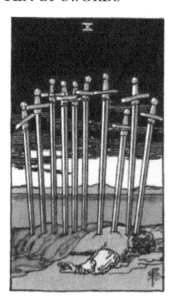

This card talks about letting go too, but from a slightly different perspective compared to its predecessor, the Nine of Swords. The Ten of Swords passes a message of succumbing to unpalatable circumstances. Many times in life, we are told to never give up, never to let ourselves be consumed by the powers of helplessness. But sometimes, we are truly helpless. In life, we try too hard to change what cannot be altered, and we only end up wearing ourselves out. Being relentless and unstoppable are good attributes, but while expending your efforts and energy towards a failing cause, sometimes, you need to take stock and see if your resources and efforts would be better suited for something else. Sometimes, admitting failure is not a bad thing in itself, it's simply an indication that you have learnt your lesson, and are ready to start afresh.

If we decide not to give up even we realize deep down that we do not stand a chance, we do not ply expend limited energy and resources, we also damage ourselves mentally. When you keep working on a failing concern instead of giving up, admitting failure and moving on, you damage your self-esteem little by little. If you do not get out in time, your image of yourself and your abilities may be so battered that achieving success in other endeavors would become incredibly difficult.

The Universal Waite Card shows a tired man; completely spent from fighting. However, the man is lying flat and swords are on his back – signifying that he has allowed himself to be conquered by forces that were simply too strong for him to handle. Life is all about growth, development and accumulating strength. It's okay to sometimes not be powerful enough to handle every single challenge that comes your way. The man looks conquered for now, but he's not dead. He has had enough of the pain for the meantime but he is waiting for the sunrise, because when the right time comes, he will stand up and move on. So, to give your mind and body the rest, respite and relief that they deserve, sometimes, you just need to give up for a while. Succumb to the forces powerful than you. Then when you have healed, rise up and keep moving.

INTRINSIC MEANING OF THE CARD: The card passes a message of surrender to the querent. When the enemy being fought is way too strong for you to handle, it is better to step back, give in, and then live to fight another day.

ACE OF PENTACLES

Live every single ace in the Minor Arcana, the Ace of Pentacles is a symbol of a moment of opportunity. The Ace of Pentacles signals a period of extreme potential and infinite possibilities; a point in time, which if properly taken advantage of, leads to immense success. The period in time indicated by the case of the pentacles is not one to be wasted or trifled with, it is a time to be extremely serious and focused, a period to be fully maximized.

The temporary nature of the fortuitous period represented by the Ace of Pentacles means that once it is gone, it may never come back. The message is simple – keep your eyes open for opportunities, and position yourself to be ready to take maximum advantage of any opportunities that come your way., Opportunities only come around once in a while, and in the blink of an eye, they are gone.

In the Universal Waite Card, a hand, representing the universe is presenting a pentacle, representing an irreplaceable opportunity. The pentacle represents a seed with lots of potential, filled with infinite possibilities. If the receiver takes maximum advantage of the seed being given to him, he would reap a bountiful harvest. The prosperous garden in the image signifies the incomparable results that the seed can bring is properly sowed and tended to. However, if an opportunity given is misused, then nothing is reaped. The saddest part is that such an opportunity may never again be regained.

In our daily lives, life presents us with several opportunities to make massive changes to our lives. Being young is an opportunity – an opportunity to pursue your goals relentlessly, a time window for you to create a better life for yourself before you get old. Being healthy is an opportunity to work as hard as you can to be comfortable and secure before sickness and frailty comes. Every day you wake up is an opportunity to make a difference, however tiny, in the world, because you will not be alive forever. So, while the Ace of Pentacles refers to huge significant opportunities that are temporary, we must keep in mind that every single day we have is an opportunity too, and we must not waste the chance we have – the chance of life.

INTRINSIC MEANING OF THE CARD: The Ace of Pentacles represents a huge opportunity for prosperity which will only be temporarily available.

TWO OF PENTACLES

This card is all about maintaining balance in life. The Two of Pentacles symbolizes those perfect moments in life where everything just makes sense – your career is going well, the home front is perfect, your investments are yielding incredible results – everything is great. Of course, challenges come in different aspects of our lives from time to time, and at times, we feel that everything is in complete chaos. The Two of Pentacles, however, represents a point in time where everything is in perfect harmony. This card also serves to remind the querent great, amazing times are coming.

In the Universal Waite Card, a ship is pictured flowing in consonance with the waves. This shows that the Two of Pentacles refers to a period of stability and harmony. Everything is flowing perfectly, and the journey of life is being silky smooth. The image of the Pentacles being juggled within the lemniscate represents the place of the divine in keeping our affairs as individuals in order. We may make spirited efforts towards keeping all aspects of our lives balanced and in perfect harmony, but the divine still plays a pretty important role in ensuring that balance and stability is maintained in all aspects of our lives.

INTRINSIC MEANING OF THE CARD: The Two of Pentacles represents balance in all aspects of life.

THREE OF PENTACLES

The Three of Pentacles symbolizes partial completion – a goal that has not been fully realized, but has begun to manifest. The Three of Pentacles simply indicates a result, an evidence of energy invested so far. Sometimes, in life, we may feel that we haven't achieved in anything, and we may be driven to despair by our belief that we have failed. The Three of Pentacles reminds us that more often than not, we are doing better than we believe, and if only we stop take stock of our achievements, we wouldn't feel so downcast.

The Three of Pentacles reminds us as individuals, of the importance of looking at how far we've come, and appreciating our own efforts. Rome wasn't built in a day, and all our goals are probably not going to be achieved at once. Some successes take time, effort and patience. So, if you feel you have not gotten to where you want to be yet, sometimes, it makes sense to appreciate how far you have actually come.

Realizing that you have more to be thankful for than to complain about puts you in a position where you are geared to achieve he rest of your goals or complete your projects. In the Universal Waite Card, three figures are shown, two of them are holding swords and written plans for a project, while the third person seems to be the one receiving the feedback about a work in progress. This image symbolizes the importance of reviewing how far we have come as individuals, and of course how much we can achieve if we put in spirited efforts into working cordially with others.

The Three of Pentacles emphasizes the importance of teamwork, and having a direction. It is one thing to have a dream, and another to actually be on a path to achieving it. Therefore, whole reviewing your success, it also important for you to check that you are still on the right path to achieving your final goal. More often than not, as humans we tend to make mistakes. Making a mistake such as losing your direction and focus and succumbing to distractions, however, is one that you cannot afford to make. Time and again, we may slip off the wagon; fall off track. However, our abilities to get right back on track after noticing our mistakes will keep us on the path to true success.

The Three of Pentacles also portrays the importance of leadership. A leader provides coordination and drive. The leader helps to keep the team together and provide direction. Therefore, whether you are serving as a leader or a follower, carrying out your responsibilities properly by directing your subordinates or following instructions to the latter is extremely crucial to long-term success.

INTRINSIC MEANING OF THE CARD: The card simply signifies the importance of reviewing goals that have begun to manifest, and the significance of teamwork and effective leadership.

FOUR OF PENTACLES

This card is all about amassing power and strength. Moving forward in life, achieving success, and overcoming obstacles all take formidable strength and a burning desire to win. However, a person doesn't just become powerful enough to tackle all the problems if life by chance. You need to work towards amassing strength. You need to surround yourself with people who make you stronger and challenge you to be even better. You need to place yourself in situations that help you to build your strength. Life is a com0lex journey that has its difficult and easy parts. So while going through the easy parts, it is important for you to reserve the energy and resources you would need to get through the difficult times.

The card does not specify the outcome of saving, but it encourages it. Reserves always come in handy, be it reserves of power, energy, money, strength or endurance. As much as possible, save up instead of spending your resources recklessly, and you will be thankful you did.

In the Universal Waite Card, focus is placed on gathering power and knowledge, as shown by the pentacle on the figure's head. The pentacle on the figure's heart indicates the importance of reserving emotional strength. Emotional and mental strength are extremely critical factors that determine whether an individual makes it through a rough point in time or not. Finally, the pentacles on the figure's feet indicate the importance of a solid foundation. Before an individual can rise to success, his foundation must be rock-solid and reliable, if not, he will fall.

Therefore, as we progress in our journey through life, we must always endeavor to check on our foundations to ensure that we do not fall and crash. The figure seems to be away from civilization, showing that go gather true strength and power, sometimes, you need to leave your comfort zone and go through difficulties. Strength is not built through pleasure; it is built through struggle.

FIVE OF PENTACLES

The five of pentacles represents being in need. Life is all about the good and the bad, and that means that sometimes we would have a lot of resources at our disposal, and sometimes, we would have none at all. While need may be critical or not, lacking needed resources is never a pleasant experience, and it puts us as individuals at the mercy of others. The Five of Pentacles communicates the message of hope and imminent help to the querent. The situation may not be rosy at the moment, but do not despair, for help is at hand. The Five of Pentacles also reminds people in need of one thing or the other that lack is temporary, and great things are coming their way soon.

Sometimes, when we require things, we get so destabilized by our intense desire for what we need that we do not pay close attention to viable opportunities right before our eyes. Therefore, this card reminds us to be on the lookout for chances of getting help while working on improving our situations.

The Universal Waite Card shows figures in need as depicted by their crutches, ragged clothing and lack of shoes even in the biting snow. This shows that being in need has the capability to take away a person's will to live, and you must always keep in mind that better days are coming. Hope is the most powerful weapon in the world, and it is the hope of finding help that's keeping these poor figures going despite their conditions.

The figures are also walking past a church, representing an opportunity for help. This passes a message to us as individuals that we must not be too consumed by our worries or by our own pride to forget to seek for help

when we need it. While in need, keep an eye out for possible sources of help and try your best to get the help that you need, In the long run, stay faithful to those who helped you and help them too when they need you.
INTRINSIC MEANING OF THE CARD: The card simply symbolizes physical need and the need to seek for help.

SIX OF PENTACLES

The Six of Pentacles is all about material energy flowing from one person to another – it's about giving to the less-privileged when you can afford it. Giving out of your own plenty or even scarce resources is a subject that has been preached about for years. Your generosity as an individual does not just impact the life of the recipient of your generosity, it greatly impacts your own life too. The balance between the giver and the receiver is delicate. Giving out is not a one-sided thing; when you gift people things, you receive an incredible feeling if happiness, fulfilment and delight in return. You have just helped someone to keep going, you have just given a person hope, and hope is the most powerful weapon in the universe.

In the Universal Waite Card, an apparently wealthy man is seen holding a set of scales in balance. The scales represent that even though he is giving out to the needy, he is not losing – he is gaining happiness and fulfillment in return.

INTRINSIC MEANING OF THE CARD: The Six of Pentacles reminds the querent of the importance of helping others out in their time of need, and signifies the joy of giving.

SEVEN OF PENTACLES

The Seven of Pentacles is all about examining and appraising the results of invested efforts. When working assiduously towards the realization of a particular goal, it is important to stop to take stock of how far you have come to ascertain the true state of your affairs. Appraisal in this context is not just to provide motivation for the querent to keep going even in spite of daunting circumstances, but also to ensure that the querent is actually still on the right path to success. As mentioned earlier in this text, it is extremely easy to deviate from one's course while working towards success. It is therefore essential for you to take a step back and examine your results so far to ensure you are still staying true to your original plan and goals.

The appraisal being discussed in this context is a means of personal judgement. You need to understand if you are actually doing the right things at all, and if you are progressing at your desired rate. Judging your own efforts and results lets you realize if an increase in your pace and efforts is needed, if you need to slow down, or if you need to devise a whole new plan of action.

The Seven of Pentacles therefore reminds us to take time off once in a while to critically and objectively quantify our progress in different aspects of our lives. How much time are you spending with your family? How many of the yearly goals that you have earmarked have been realized? Objective appraisal lets you realize where you need to intensify your efforts, and how.

In the Universal Waite Card, a man is shown critically examining pentacles growing on a vine. He is calm, curious and serious. This represents the best form of effort appraisal – a form of appraisal that employs the principles of curiosity and absolute seriousness. It is your life quite alright, but you owe it to yourself, the ones who believe in you, and the divine who granted you your life to make the most of it. Still in the image, a prosperous, bountiful harvest is shown.

Despite the obviously amazing results of his efforts, the man does not get over-excited, he still calmly examines each individual result. This signifies that it doesn't matter how amazingly you think you are performing; you still need to initiate checks and balances to ensure you improve on your already amazing results.

INTRINSIC CARD MEANING: The Seven of Pentacles simply communicates the message of constant personal appraisal to ensure steady growth and development.

EIGHT OF PENTACLES

The Eight of Pentacles symbolizes the importance of hard work and diligence. More often than not, we hear it in life that the single most important and most controllable factor influencing success is hard work. In this case, life is extremely simple; what you give is what you get. If you invest the necessary efforts, you get your desired results, most of the time.

It is, however, worthy of mention, that it is not all the time that hard work pays. Sometimes, as individuals, in different aspects of our lives, we may find ourselves working hard towards the realization if a goal that eventually does not come to fruition. It is therefore extremely important never to give up even in the face of failure and to keep pressing on.

Hard work is also not the only factor dictating success – efficient planning, an amazing network, and sufficient knowledge also play important roles in success. The key thing to note about the Eight of Pentacles, however, is if you do not work for it, you will probably not achieve it.

The Eight of Pentacles also highlights the importance of consistency and assiduous repetition. Hard work is useless without consistency. Whatever efforts you are putting into an endeavor; you are required to be consistent with them. Do not be the type that works hard only 2 times out of 5 attempts. Be the reliable individual who always gives his all. Remember if it is worth doing at all, then it is worth doing well.

In the Universal Waite Card, an image of a Craftsman turning a pentacle over repeatedly is shown. Even though the pentacle being observed does not seem defective, the craftsman is still examining it critically to ensure that no mistake has been made in its creation. The craftsman's dedication and commitment to excellence represents a habit that we must strive to inculcate in our everyday lives as individuals. Do not just be contented with being average because settling for less is a habit that breeds mediocrity. Make excellence your watchword and pursue it relentlessly at all times.

INTRINSIC MEANING OF THE CARD: The Eight of Pentacles signifies the importance of diligence, hard work and a commitment to excellence.

NINE OF PENTACLES

The Nine of Pentacles indicates success and glory, simply. This card illustrates the joy that comes with working hard an endeavor or a task for so long, and eventually achieving success. This card is not about the external validation and recognition that success attracts, it is about the personal feeling of accomplishment and contentment that comes with starting a task and successfully finishing to achieve desired results. The feeling is truly incomparable.

The Nine of Pentacles signifies the product of discipline, hard work and dedication. The simple, yet hard truth is that in a society where a lot of people are settling for an average existence, striving to be spectacular can be immensely difficult. Therefore, trying harder than everybody to be excellent, and finally achieving success, is a truly remarkable feeling.

In the Universal Waite Card, the glory of success achieved through hard work and dedication is illustrated. A well-dressed woman is pictured in a luxuriant, blossoming garden. The beauty and prosperity of the garden signifies the results of months or years of cultivating flowers and trees, tending to them and growing them to become beautiful and remarkable. In the same vein, true success is not achieved in a day; it is a result of years of pursuing a particular goal relentlessly.

The falcon in the image symbolizes discipline. Discipline is a critical factor dictating success that is closely related to hard work. If you are not disciplined you cannot work hard, at least not consistently. Self-discipline keeps you on the path to your goals and enables you to resist distractions that would only make you deviate from the path to success. The grapevines

in the picture have been said to represent hard work. Working hard helps sets you apart from the others and positions you on a direct route to success, provided you remain dedicated and consistent with your efforts.
INTRINSIC MEANING OF THE CARD: The card simply symbolizes the joy of glory that has been earned.

TEN OF PENTACLES

This card represents wealth, abundance and prosperity – the overall goal of life. The ace of pentacles represents an opportunity; a period in time laden with potential and promise; the Ten of Pentacles represents a manifestation of that promise. The card signifies financial stability and security. You have worked very hard consistently over a long period of time, and you have achieved remarkable success. You have not just achieved one single accomplishment – you have been severally and repeatedly successful in a lot of undertakings as a result of you being alert to opportunities, being hardworking, consistent, dedicated and committed to excellence instead of settling for mediocrity. So where other people are living average lives, you enjoy true happiness and stupendous fortune.

The Ten of Cards does not just represent having a lot of money or bang famously rich; it represents building a legacy that transcends one's existence. You have succeeded in creating a name that would not be tarnished, a name that will carry on for generations after you. You have constructed an empire. The card is about looking back at your accomplishments with pride and being appreciative of all you have achieved.

You have worked hard and stayed committed to your aspirations, and finally, you have made it; your struggles have paid off. The card is also about reflecting on the beauty of the present, and taking time to relish your current accomplishments. You have done well for yourself, and you have earned the luxury of admiring the results of your own hard work. While it is critical not to get too pompous, it is still essential to appreciate how far you have come.

Finally, the card also signifies hope for an even brighter and grander future. Even as a successful individual, you do not get to rest on your oars. You are allowed to take a break to relish your success, and then get back to work to further consolidate on your achievements. Success is never fully achieved; you keep working harder to attain even bigger levels of success. This card, therefore, symbolizes looking ahead into the future with supreme confidence and self-assurance. You have come this far, and you still have more to achieve.

In the Universal Waite Card, a young couple is pictured in the center, reflecting the beauty of the present. A child represents the future, and an older man represents the past. The image signifies the relationship between these three points in time, and how they all come together to deeply influence our lives, decisions and actions. The past influences our present, and both the actions of the past and the present determine the brightness or bleakness of the future.

The dogs in the picture signify the values of devotion and loyalty. Dogs are extremely allegiant creatures – they stay faithful and committed to their owners, standing by them relentlessly through thick and thin. To be truly successful and remain successful, inculcating the values of faithfulness and loyalty is extremely critical. Being faithful to deserving people, to a cause, and to a dream are important to success.

People would serve as your rungs on your ladder to success, and you never know when you would need someone again. So in all you, remain loyal to the ones who stood by you. If you are not committed to your dreams on the other hand, derailing from your path becomes possible, and that is something you cannot afford. Therefore, it is important for you to keep your goas in focus and block out all distractions.

The pentacles, banners and the arch all symbolize regality and lasting, enduring wealth. You have achieved success, and repeatedly proven yourself as dedicated and committed to your goals. You have consolidated on your many successes, and now you march on to discover new frontiers of wealth and prosperity.

INTRINSIC MEANING OF THE CARD: The Ten of Pentacles signifies true, enduring wealth and riches.

COURT CARDS

The court cards are the final 16 cards of the Minor Arcana suit, and they symbolize people, or more aptly, they symbolize the roles played by specific people in our lives. In the olden days of Tarot reading, readers and querents tried to deduce the exact person in a querent's life that a court card referred to. That is not necessary anymore, however. Once the card is read, the interpretation may be used to figure out the role the individual in question plays in relation to the question asked by the querent.

Using roles played by individuals in different aspects of our lives to interpret Court card readings makes it even more convenient to take necessary action in the situation or circumstance in which the question was asked.

The Court Cards consist of four different characters, each of which feature in the Wands, Cups, Swords and Pentacles suits. The different characters that make up the Court Cards are the Page, the Knight, the Queen, and the King.

PAGES

A page card symbolizes a person who requires help or guidance to find his feet in a particular situation. In many situations, a page may be interpreted as a novice or a newbie who has suddenly found himself thrust into a whole new system or place. He does not understand how the new situation he is in works yet, and he requires all the sincere help and direction he can get.

The nature of the page is characterized by a mix of excitement and fear. He is exhilarated at the opportunity to be a part of something new and thrilling, but at the same time, he is scared of losing his way, making a mistake or finding out that the new system just doesn't suit him. Therefore, for the page to cope, he needs to be constantly supervised, monitored and encouraged. The page is also characterized by curiosity and a deep burning desire to learn.

The page is new to the system and knows next to nothing about it – he is itching to know as much as he can about the new system, and he is trying to determine if the organization is actually the best fit for him. A page is therefore in his exploratory phase, and has probably not made a choice yet.

Due to the fact that the page is still a newbie trying to find out if the new system us actually the best fit for him, he may have issues with commitment and dedication. If he finds out that he might not thrive or flourish in the system he has found himself, he might abscond and venture off to explore new opportunities. The page does not have any deep connections with the system or organization and he is only trying to figure out exactly what is best for him.

Pages are also usually not very influential or powerful; they do not command a lot of authority. The page is newbie, sort of like an intern. In the hierarchy of this system, he probably ranks quite low. Therefore, he might not have the power to make important decisions or even influence any important events. The actions or inactions of a page may therefore not have any serious effects on a querent's life. The page is, however, a helpful and supportive character.

The page is an individual trying to learn as much as possible. He supports and assists as much as he can to gain favor in the eyes of the ones who matter, and of course to really determine if he is in the best place for him. The page is also a very eager character. He is not just eager to learn, he is eager to practice, to experiment, to be seen and heard. His eagerness and zealousness makes him a seemingly weak, yet integral part of any team, especially in the role of providing needed assistance that does not require immense skill or experience.

Finally, the page is prone to mistakes. He does not know his left from his right yet, and he is only experimenting with activities. Therefore, he would be grateful for any kind of direction or sincere advice he can get on how to become better. The page is an individual who may have formidable potential, but still requires refinement and education to succeed.

There are four classes of Pages – the Page of Wands, the Page of Cups, the Page of Swords. and the Page of Pentacles. All the pages have similar characteristics as they have been described above, they only differ in the capacities in which they operate in, or the realms and circumstances in which they are found.

THE PAGE OF WANDS

This page possesses the power of will and determination that the Wands are renowned for. Therefore, the Page of Wands refers to a young or new individual to a system just discovering himself and his passions. He has not grasped the full extent of his own potential or capabilities, nut he is driven by determination and sheer passion. He may not know what he wants yet, but he is determined to find his way.

In the Universal Waite Card, the Page of Wands is shown holding the wand at a distance, showing that he is still considering possibilities and paths through which to channel his brimming energy. The Page of Wands is determined to succeed, but is still exploring different opportunities.

INTRINSIC MEANING OF THE CARD: An individual who is still finding his feet, and is driven by will and determination.

THE PAGE OF CUPS

The Page of Cups is similar to the Page of Wands, except that he operates in the realm of emotions, relationships and creativity. He is still finding his feet in a new relationship, or learning how to handle new, strange emotions. Instead of diving right into the new situation or possibility, he is simply exploring and considering his chances.

In the Universal Waite Card, the fish peeking out of the Cup represents the partial understanding that the page has of the complicated nature of emotions and relationships. The Cup is held at arm's length, indicating that the page is not committing himself to any cause yet – he is only considering and studying a particular option for the meantime.

INTRINSIC MEANING OF THE CARD: An individual trying to figure out his chances in the realm of emotions, relationships and creativity.

THE PAGE OF SWORDS

The Page of Swords represents a newbie experimenting with new methods of communication, new ideas and new ramifications of thought. Just like all other pages, he is only examining and regarding the new entity, he is not fully accepting or refuting it yet.

In the Universal Waite Card, the Page is seen examining a new sword. He attempts to get a feel of a sword, to see if it suits him. He is not choosing or rejecting the sword, he is just trying to see if it might eventually be his choice.

INTRINSIC MEANING OF THE CARD: An individual experimenting with new ideas, knowledge and problem-solving techniques.

THE PAGE OF PENTACLES

This card refers to an individual who has just gained access to a new resource, material item or an opportunity that could lead to wealth. The Page of Pentacles is a man of potential and high intelligence; and he actually has the requirements to convert the opportunity being given to him into immense wealth and prosperity. However, he is not delving blindly into anything serious yet. He is carefully juggling his options in his mid, trying to find out which path would be the best fit for his abilities. The Page of Pentacles may or may not succeed, but he is definitely going to make a spirited attempt.

In the Universal Waite Card, the Page is seen examining a pentacle. He holds it carefully, trying to not to destroy it or ruin the immense value it possesses. The Page regards the pentacle closely, marveling at the spectacular possibilities the Pentacle can provide. However, like all pages, he hasn't made a choice. He is only researching.

THE KNIGHTS

The Knight is a step above the page. He does not have a lot of authority or influence, but he is strong, fast and may be considerably dangerous. The Knight is characterized by rapid, and sometimes rash actions and decisions. One of the golden qualities of a Knight is his intense focus. The Knight is completely obsessed about his desires and goals, and would go the ends of the world to accomplish them.

The Knight gets so fixated on a goal that he completely forgets and neglects everything else in his mad pursuit of his goals. He tends to be extreme, unpredictable and quite difficult control. So, while the Knight may be lethally effective and hardworking individual to have on a team, he may destroy the entire team's efforts with his rashness and lack of decorum.

If the Knight can be properly cautioned and positioned on a productive path, however, he would unleash all his passion and determination on the cause at hand, and pursue it to a logical conclusion, even if it is the last thing he ever does. The Knight is insanely committed to his cause, and never backs down.

If a Knight is on your team and you can get him to channel his infinite energy towards a productive task, he is guaranteed to over deliver as long as he is truly passionate and motivated about the cause in question. If a Knight is against you and has set his mind on destroying you however, he can be a very difficult and formidable adversary for one single reason – he will not back down. Now, let's dig into the Knights of the various suits of the Minor Arcana.

KNIGHT OF WANDS

The Knight of Wands is an obsessive individual who actions are powered by will and determination. The Knight of Wands combines the obsessive desire for a goal of a Knight and the power of will and passion characteristic of the Wands suit, to form a dangerously effective single entity. The Knight of Wands has a specific goal, and whatever it takes, he will achieve it. He is either a powerful asset or a dangerous adversary. If he is against you, take care of him first, or else, he is going to cause you serious problems. It is easy to overlook a knight because he seems average in influence, but his insanely relentless attitude makes him extremely dangerous. The intensity and vigor of the Knight of Wands is not always long-lasting, however. Eventually, the fire in him begins to die down and he runs out of steam. He is the type that tends to go fast and crash, especially if not controlled.

In the Universal Waite Card, a figure is pictured on a horse facing a particular direction. The horse is advancing dangerously fast, and has one goal – making it to the required destination. The horse rears perilously, signifying the limited self-control and restraint that the Knight of Wands has.

Universal Waite Card: The Knight of Cards signifies a person who relentlessly and recklessly pursues a goal he is passionate about.

KNIGHT OF CUPS

Where the Knight of Wands is riled up by will and passion, the Knight of Cups operates in the realm of emotions, inspiration and creativity. The Knight of Cups may be in the quest to achieve a vision, a creation of his own, or to win the love of his life. Nothing else matters but his dream, and he will do anything to get what he wants. He is a very difficult person to dissuade from a quest, and he is likely to run you down if you do not stay out of his way. If your dreams and visions align with his, he may be a very formidable tool to your success if you learn how to help him curb his excesses.

In the Universal Waite Card, the Knight of Cups is shown moving slowly but firmly towards his goal. He is obviously a lot more controlled than the Knight of Wands, but he is just as fiercely determined to achieve his goal. He has a firm grasp of reality and keeps his vision in focus at all times; it is what drives him to keep going forward despite all obstacles in his path.

INTRINSIC MEANING OF THE CARD: The Knight of Cups is an individual who relentlessly pursues a vision, a creative ambition, or a love interest.

KNIGHT OF SWORDS

The Knight of Swords is motivated by logic, ideas and belief systems. All that matters to him is his beliefs and ideas. Once he believes in something, he will go to the ends of the earth to advance the cause of that belief or to defend it. The Knight of Swords is an extremely committed individual, and may constantly use his superb communication skills for the advancement of his cause.

Like all other Knights the Knight of Swords is obstinate and unrelenting in the pursuit of his goals, and he may have dangerous tendencies. He moves fast and flounders dangerously, but he still keeps his goals in focus. He requires constant external control to be truly effective.

In the Universal Waite Card, the Knight of Swords is only shown as a blur of fast and determined movement. He advances dangerously fast towards his goal, and his momentum is fueled by his personal convictions. His wildly swung swords indicates his minimal restraint and possible lack of a strategy. He just presses forward, and usually acts before thinking.

INTRINSIC MEANING OF THE CARD: A powerful and motivated individual who works towards the advancement of a belief or idea.

KNIGHT OF PENTACLES

The Knight of Pentacles is motivated by wealth, material items and physical resources. In short, he relentlessly chases riches.

In the Universal Waite Card, the horse of the Knight of Pentacles is motionless and poised – indicating stability and purpose. The Knight of Pentacles is well trained and has learnt to control some of his impulses. He is pictured waiting for the right moment to strike. Like all other knights however, his focus is lasered directly on his goal, and that's the only thing on his mind, He may be static at the moment, but as soon as the right moment strikes, he will pounce.

INTRINSIC MEANING OF THE CARD: An individual powerfully motivated by wealth and prosperity.

QUEENS

The Queen plays a supportive yet influential role. The Queen operates in the capacity of assisting a more powerful individual, but she has the ability to sway his decisions and influence his actions. The Queen represents the subtle yet commanding power of a woman – she operates in the shadows but exerts considerable influence. The Queen also represents a motherly-like character who is willing to help and advice, provided that the querent's cause is one she believes in. She has more power than she lets on, and she has the ability to create and to destroy without anyone knowing what she has done.

The Queen, like the knight is a very powerful, albeit more controlled and discreet ally, and a devastating adversary. If you dare oppose or betray her, she will use all the forces at her disposal to crush you, and you will not see it coming. The Queen is not often recognized for the critical role she plays in the maintenance of stability and prosperity, so she enjoys being appreciated and recognized for her indisputably important duties.

QUEEN OF WANDS

The Queen of Wands is a powerful yet secretive and usually unnoticed individual who is motivated by will and determination. If she is passionate about a cause, she will use her clandestine powers to influence decisions to work in her favor. If she senses that your passion aligns with hers, she can be a very powerful adviser and inspiration.

In the Universal Waite Card, the Queen of Wands is portrayed as a mildly masculine, confident and assertive figure. She is fiercely determined, and will get what she wants, not by force and confrontation, but by guile and pulling important strings. The sunflower in the picture represents optimism – she is positive that her powerful connections will get her what she wants. The black cat in the image represents the Queen's powerful intuition and her ability to sense danger and opportunity when others don't. By looking into the distance, the Queen is scanning for chances and opportunities to advance her own cause and passions.

QUEEN OF CUPS

The Queen of Cups is a secretly powerful individual rarely acknowledged for her powers in the realm of emotions, creativity and relationships. The Queen of cups plays the role of an adviser and an experienced tutor in the intricate fields of emotions, creativity and relationships. She has grown to learn that logic does not always cut it when it comes to the issues of the heart, and she gives superb emotional guidance using her extremely efficient intuition. The Queen of Cups reminds the querent to follow his heart and take a risk for once.

In the Universal Waite Card, the figure in the image is seen deeply and critically observing an elaborate chalice. This represents the experience the Queen of Cups has in the delicate business of emotions and relationships. She had had personal experience, and she has helped a lot of people navigate the tricky waters of emotions, but she still finds the gripping power of feelings and inspiration deeply mesmerizing. Emotions are the only thing in the world that can make a person deliberately take a wrong step. The heart simply just wants what it wants.

The Queen of Cups is also pictured above the water in the image. This indicates her objectivity and ability to understand complicated situations die to her intuition and experience. She can distance herself from the issue at hand and the people in question and give reasonable practicable advice. Even though she is deeply intuitive, the Queen of Cups is experienced enough to never allow her emotions to cloud her sense of judgment.

INTRINSIC MEANING OF THE CARD: The Queen of Cups represents a subtly influential individual who guides and directs other people in the world of emotions, relationships and creativity.

QUEEN OF SWORDS

Just like all other Queens in the Court cards, the Queen of swords wields a clandestine yet powerful influence, and she plays the motherly role of guiding and directing people. This Queen, however, operates in the territory of ideas, communications and strategy. She is all about beliefs and thoughts. She is intelligent and experienced, and has powerful personal convictions. She is deeply logical and extremely organized.

When she has a plan that needs to be carried out, she organizes her steps from the first to the last even before starting at all. She is a master in the art of strategy and she solves delicate and complex problems with ease. She uses diverse communication methods she has mastered over time to influence others to do her bidding.

In the Universal Waite Card, the Queen of Swords sits above the clouds – representing a clear and unclouded mind that reasons lucidly and creates reliable plans and strategies. She believes strongly in a cause, and allows her conviction to drive her actions. The birds and butterflies in the image signify her remarkable and well-thought out intentions. She has plans, and she is determined to achieve them using her own secret powers.

INTRINSIC MEANING OF THE CARD: The Queen of Swords represents a powerful and organized individual who advices and assists in the territory of ideas, logic and decision-making.

THE QUEEN OF PENTACLES

The Queen of the Pentacles is a lot like the other Queens of the court cards, but she gives advice about achieving results, maximizing opportunities and amassing wealth. The Queen of Pentacles is all about acquiring wealth and making the best use of limited resources. She is a master at crafting out plans that help individuals start out from the scratch right up to prosperity. She's usually a wealthy and powerful person herself, but she keeps her influence hidden and mentors the people she believes in.

The Queen of Pentacles pays a lot of attention to detail, and is always extremely thorough with her plans and advice. She is also an expert fixer. She finds a way to remedy even the worst situations and place selected individuals who have fallen off the rails back on the track of prosperity again.

In the Universal Waite Card, the Queen of Pentacles is pictured sitting in a luxurious, opulent garden filled with signs of bounty and prosperity. She has worked hard to create a haven of wealth for herself, and she now helps others achieve what she has amassed. The rabbit in the image symbolizes fertility – she grows ideas into success stories. The earth and water in the image are representations of abundance. Wherever the Queen of Pentacles goes, abundance and prosperity follow her because she never compromises in her principles, and they always work.

INTRINSIC MEANING OF THE CARD: The Queen if Pentacles represents an individual who assists, nurtures and advices in the world of resource management, financial stability and personal growth.

KINGS

This group of cards represents the apex individuals in the various realms – will, emotions, logic and wealth. These individuals have legitimate power and authority and they have the influence to greatly affect the querent's life in one way or the other, The King makes top-tier decisions, delegates responsibilities to his subordinates and ins generally responsible for coordinating people below him while maintaining order and stability in his domain.

The King is usually a master in his field, He does not just become King by chance, he has been working assiduously for a long time, and he has rightfully earned his place at the top. He is a true expert in his own turf, and exerts absolute influence. His decision more often than not, is final.

Gaining access to a King is not easy. He is not only extremely bust; he is also usually well-protected and inaccessible to the average person. To get to meet the King, you need to make spirited efforts and have an acceptable reason. The King is also not likely to be easily overpowered or influenced against his will. He may be convinced, but he cannot be forced.

KING OF WANDS

The King of Wands is an authority that operates based on his passions and personal motivation. The King of Wand is a highly motivated and driven individual who exerts a lot of influence in the territory he rules over. He is not emotional – he is cold, and he is stirred by his goals and desires only. To get the attention or approval of the King of Wands, the querent has to show the alignment between his passion and the King's ambitions, and show how his involvement in the King's plans can further the advancement of the King's passions.

In the Universal Waite Card, the King of Wands is trying as hard as possible to remain seated – he is an active and constantly motivated individual. His burning passions consume him and fuel him to accomplish more. His energy and desires, however, predispose him to making hasty decisions.

INTRINSIC MEANING OF THE CARD: The King of Wands represents an individual who has the authority to command and rule his personal domain, and is driven by passion and sheer will.

KING OF CUPS

Unlike the King of Wands, the King of Cups is driven by his emotions. He is calm and collected, but he is not stone cold. He is compassionate and tolerant without being easily swayed. To gain his attention and favor, the querent must appeal to his compassionate and merciful side, because that's the side that most controls his actions.

In the Universal Waite Card, the King is seen calmly regarding the cup in his hand. He does not seem extremely excited or fazed by the influence he wields – he is an experienced ruler who takes his duties seriously, but does not see power as anything unusual anymore. The King is shown to move smoothly and confidently across the surface of the water – he is neither scared nor anxious. This shows the ability of the King of Cups to remain stable and steady even in the most volatile situations. The fish and the boat in the image represent the emotional and logical sides of the King respectively. He manages to strike a delicate balance between the two, ensuring that while he is being compassionate, he still keeps his thoughts clear and his judgement unbiased.

INTRINSIC MEANING OF THE CARD: The King of Cups represents an individual who has considerable influence in his territory, and is driven by emotions, relationships and inspiration.

KING OF SWORDS

The King of Swords is driven by his ideas, beliefs and personal convictions. He makes his decisions based on logic, rather than emotions, and he is the least likely of the Kings to be swayed by an emotional plea or an argument that appeals to his sense of compassion. He is a master of strategy and organization, and works hard to keep his empire running. He is all about long-term stability and survival, and if you can get him to believe in your idea, or if you can present a proposal that aligns with his personal convictions, then you will have his attention.
The King of Swords, like all other Sword characters is obsessed with preparedness and strategy, He is always ready for any eventuality, and he plans his moves all the way to the end, He is never caught by surprise and works assiduously to pursue his plans to a logical conclusion.
In the Universal Waite Card, the King of Swords is shown with a sword in his hand symbolizing his core principles of honesty and fairness. He does not tolerate cheating or corruption. He holds himself to a very high standard, and he expects those who follow him to be scrupulous and truthful in all their dealings too. As stated earlier, he is heavily influenced by his own personal convictions and principles. His experience and ideologies help him to make the best decisions and solve even the most complicated of problems. He sticks to a code, and never departs from it.
INTRINSIC MEANING OF THE CARD: The card symbolizes an individual with power and absolute authority who is driven by his beliefs, ideas and convictions.

KING OF PENTACLES

The King of Pentacles is an influential authority that is practical, result-oriented, and driven by wealth, prosperity and stability. The primary aim of the King of Pentacles is to see his empire flourish under his watch. He is efficient, and a master of investment and resource management. He is swayed by material items and the promise of abundance. That does not mean he can be bribed with money, but it signifies that a plan that can bring additional prosperity to his domain would be a great way to capture his attention.

In the Universal Waite Card, the King of Pentacles is seen to be surrounded by resources. He is prosperous, and his overgrown garden shows that he manages not only his own wealth, but the wealth of the system that he controls. He wears expensive, soft-looking clothes, but his impenetrable armor is visible underneath. This shows that while might be primarily driven by seeking abundance and wealth, he can still be firm and principled, and is not to be trifled with. If he notices any dissident trying to sabotage his efforts at improving the state of his empire, he weeds such a person out ruthlessly. Nothing stands between the King of Pentacles and his desires.

INTRINSIC MEANING OF THE CARD: The King of Pentacles represents an authority that is driven primarily by wealth creation and long-term prosperity and stability of his domain.

FINAL NOTES

Like every field of knowledge, tarot is extremely expansive. There is still so much more to be learnt, so endeavor to learn even more. This book is meant to be your foundation, and not an exhaustive source of information about tarot reading as an art. I'm therefore using this opportunity to enjoin you not to just read this book and forget about it. If it's been worth reading, then it is now worth being put into practice. Hone your reading and interpretation skills, and evolve your own style as you grow. Journal heartily and sincerely, as this will help you remember everything you learn even more clearly. As stated severally in the book, tarot is an art and a science. You can create your own unique perspective to reading the cards, as long as you do not violate the fundamental rules.

A great idea that has worked for me, and helped me to remain conversant with tarot interpretations over the years, is constantly sharing my knowledge with other people. Discussing the various interpretations of the cards with like minds and even skeptics can help you gain more insight into the actual meanings of the cards. Also, do not forget to have fun with tarot – it can be a very exciting hobby. From your rituals to your journals, keep everything light-hearted and just enjoy every step of the process.

It's been great having you on this rather lengthy journey. Now, go forth, and inspire!

Made in the USA
Monee, IL
25 February 2020